SERVICE LEARNING

in Grades K–8

To Bridget Meer, who never met a kid she didn't love

To the staff of the ADAPEP program, who have taught me, inspired me, and amazed me for over 16 years with their dedication, persistence, creativity, and belief in the resiliency of the kids with whom they work
It has been my pleasure to work with you!

SERVICE LEARNING

in Grades K–8

Experiential Learning That Builds Character and Motivation

KATE THOMSEN

Foreword by Shelley Billig

CORWIN PRESS
A SAGE Publications Company
Thousand Oaks, California

For information:

Corwin Press
A Sage Publications Company
2455 Teller Road
Thousand Oaks, California 91320
www.corwinpress.com

Sage Publications Ltd.
1 Oliver's Yard
55 City Road
London EC1Y 1SP
United Kingdom

Sage Publications India Pvt. Ltd.
B-42, Panchsheel Enclave
Post Box 4109
New Delhi 110 017 India

Printed in the United States of America

Library of Congress Cataloging-in-Publication Data

Thomsen, Kate.
Service-learning in grades K-8: Experiential learning that builds character and motivation/Kate Thomsen.
     p.cm.
Includes bibliographical references and index.
ISBN 1–4129–1342-X (cloth)—ISBN 1–4129–1343–8 (pbk.)
   1. Student service. 2. Experiential learning. 3. Moral education. I. Title.
LC220.5.T46 2006
361.3'7—dc22   2005009910

This book is printed on acid-free paper.

05   06   07   08   09   10   9   8   7   6   5   4   3   2   1

Acquisitions Editor:	Rachel Livsey
Editorial Assistant:	Phyllis Cappello
Typesetter:	C&M Digitals (P) Ltd.
Proofreader:	Scott Oney
Indexer:	Rick Hurd
Cover Designer:	Michael Dubowe

Contents

Foreword

The American education system exists to prepare young people to develop the knowledge, skills, and disposition to succeed in life. Too often, though, the system fails to meet the needs of all children and youth. For a large variety of reasons, educators often feel compelled to use instructional methods that engage only some of the children, try to cover all the material in a textbook instead of focusing on teaching the most important subject matter for students to learn, and focus on students' knowledge rather than skills and disposition development.

Some educators, though, are willing to take the risk of doing things a different way. These educators recognize that people learn best when they are appropriately challenged, when they have a way to connect new knowledge and skills with things they already know, and when they can see that what they learn has utility in real life. These educators do not abandon standards or assessments, but rather, take them as a given and look for the best pedagogies to capture the attention of all their students and provide students with multiple ways of learning.

Many educators who embrace this philosophy have found that service-learning is one of the instructional methods that serves young people best. Service-learning is an approach that facilitates students' learning of academic standards through engaging them in providing service that meets real community needs. Young people may build a playground as a way to learn geometry, measurement, or other mathematics skills. They may examine statistics that show that local infant mortality is connected with poor nutrition in homeless shelters and pubic housing units, and initiate a campaign to provide nutritional information for new parents in doctors' offices and clinics and free vitamin enriched infant formula for those in need. Students may have seen injuries caused by poor traffic control by their schools, investigate how to get the city to install traffic lights, and develop a strategy to convince officials to do so. They may see the need to capture the stories of World War II from local seniors who fought in the war, and by writing interview questions and developing multimedia presentations for other students, help history come alive for themselves and others. They may see younger students in need of tutoring to learn reading skills or in need of a model to show them how to work with disabled persons. The list of needs is endless, and students who are given the opportunity generally are creative in identifying what they can do to provide service that enables them to master the standards in the curriculum. For educators, service-learning just takes the will to do it, a little time, and the willingness to let students take more control of their own learning.

As a researcher in the field of service-learning, I have learned firsthand about what participation in high-quality service-learning can do for students. At RMC Research Corporation, we have done studies that show there are positive outcomes for students, community members, and educators.

First, depending on the nature of the service-learning activities, students tend to derive academic, career, social, and civic benefits. The academic benefits come because students are more engaged in their learning and tend to see the value that school can bring. Their engagement is cognitive (they want to learn the subject matter), affective (they like school and the subject matter better), and behavioral (they do what they are asked to do). This engagement, in turn, helps students to acquire knowledge and skills related to the content standards. However, service-learning is associated more often with the acquisition of higher-order skills such as problem solving, perspective taking, and analysis, than with the more basic ones. That is because service-learning, when conducted well, asks students to become involved with identifying a community need, providing evidence that the need exists, brainstorming multiple ways to meet the need, selecting from among alternatives, implementing the solution to the problem, and seeing the literal consequences of their choices. Service-learning is deeper, tends to be remembered longer, and is more easily transferred to other settings than are other forms of learning.

Students also tend to develop strong relationships with their peers who are engaged in the service with them and with adults other than their teachers and parents. This relational aspect of service-learning meets the developmental needs of young people, particularly those in middle school and high school, and provides them with an avenue to form a strong relationship with a caring adult who may serve as a role model for both behavior and ethics. RMC Research Corporation's studies show that young people frequently experience a strong sense of efficacy when engaged in service-learning because they feel that they are making a difference in solving a problem. These studies also find that from service-learning, students become more attached to their schools and communities and more likely to show pride in these settings and take on greater responsibility for the well-being of others. They learn more about possible careers through the adults they meet during their service and in the research and presentation activities that are often associated with the service-learning tasks.

Young people also tend to become more civic-minded as a result of service-learning. They are often better able to see the ways in which our democracy works, their roles and responsibilities within it, and both their power to make a difference and the need to respect others and the laws and policies that govern our collective behavior. Students learn firsthand how decisions are made, how teaming occurs, how social issues are addressed, and the results of social action. They may learn about justice, government, and fairness. They see the world as being bigger than just their own place within it.

Community members benefit, not just from having needs met but from establishing stronger bonds with youth and with school systems. These bonds tend to change the nature of these relationships, with community members often remarking how valuable young people can be as resources and how important their opinions about life and the community are in understanding how to shape the future. Community members also tend to become more supportive of schools, since they see the challenges and strengths of the educational system.

In addition, teachers and administrators tend to benefit from service-learning through experiencing the energy and motivation of the young people and the need to reexamine the pedagogies in use in order to produce the deepest and broadest learning. Service-learning often prompts discussions among faculty about how young people learn best, how instruction can be differentiated, how to capitalize on students' strengths, how to scaffold learning, and how to make learning engaging and meaningful. Many of the most successful teachers talk about how they had to learn to let go, giving students more choices but also more responsibility for their own learning. Those teachers who were able to find the right combination of structure and choice said that they would never go back to teaching the way they did before they tried service-learning.

The story is not all rosy, though. Service-learning only produces these results when it is implemented with high quality. Low-quality service-learning has no yield in any of the ways outlined—none at all.

What is high-quality service-learning? Studies at RMC Research Corporation show that high quality is associated with four service-learning implementation strategies. First, service-learning must be linked to standards. Without a strong, intentional link, service-learning does not produce the type of knowledge and skills that the curriculum calls for. This link can be forged more deeply when students are made aware of the particular standards that need to be mastered through the service-learning experience.

Second, students need to have direct contact with those being served. At RMC Research Corporation, we have found that such personal relationships are important and make a deep impression on those providing service. When students talk with those who benefit from the service, students tend to derive more benefit themselves and the relationship becomes mutually rewarding. In addition, service then has a human face and is seen by students as more complex and more fulfilling.

Third, the service-learning reflection activities must be cognitively challenging. Teachers cannot simply ask students to write something in their journals describing their experiences. Rather, students should be required to engage in multiple types of reflection (such as nonlinguistic representations of their experiences, tying the experiences in with content standards, and providing explicit analysis of solution sets) and to employ other advanced thinking skills (such as evaluation, critique, analysis, synthesis, and inference). Teachers know how to elicit this work: They simply need to be more intentional and thoughtful about weaving these skills into the reflection and demonstration of knowledge activities.

Finally, the service-learning activities should involve youth voice and choice. Young people must have the opportunity to make decisions, see the consequences of their actions, and make decisions to improve their own processes. Ideally, young people are taught how to assess community needs through mapping or other strategies, debate the needs to be tackled, develop explicit decision-making criteria, make choices, and evaluate the consequences of their actions.

Shelley H. Billig
Vice President, RMC Research Corporation

Preface

Can you remember an exceptionally good day from your own school experience? Is there at least one day that you will always remember? What was it about that day that was so special? I am willing to guess that it was a day when you accomplished something very important. Maybe someone important, like a teacher, asked you to do something for her or him, or for someone else, and you felt special because that teacher thought of you. It was then that you most likely knew that you really mattered. Or maybe someone, like a classmate, noticed that you were really good at something. Isn't it amazing that after all these years memories like that are so fresh? That is because people often forget what we say and do, but they never forget how we make them feel (Carerra, 1999). Can you imagine leaving school without ever having had an exceptionally good and memorable experience? I wonder how many kids do leave without such an experience. All kids, from those who graduate with honors to those who struggle to graduate, need to leave school with empowering memories. Service-learning is a teaching strategy that can give kids exceptionally good and memorable experiences, among many other positive things.

WHO IS THIS BOOK WRITTEN FOR? ◼

This book is written for the teachers and other educators who believe that their students deserve learning experiences that motivate and engage them, as well as prepare them for their future role as citizens. It is for educators who know that when they are talking about the art of teaching, one size does not fit all. It is for educators who are ready to try something different but not necessarily new, since service-learning has its roots in the educational philosophy of John Dewey. While Dewey (1916) did not advocate for service-learning by name, he did believe that education ought to be experiential and related to citizenship.

Service-learning has been described by various authors and organizations in many different ways. This book will clarify what service-learning is, what it does for *all* students, and how teachers and other educators can get started with it in their own schools and classrooms. Chapter 1 discusses the benefits of service-learning for all students, and Chapter 2 assists the reader in understanding the research documenting those benefits from a practical point of view. Chapter 3 helps readers see that infusing the Essential Elements of Effective Service-Learning into existing projects is very doable. Chapter 4 provides the basics of laying the groundwork for getting started with service-learning, and Chapter 5 offers specific examples of team-building and reflection activities, two key features of quality service-learning projects. Chapters 6 and 7 provide ideas for service-learning projects, along with specifics on how to adapt them for specific situations. Chapter 8 discusses sustaining service-learning once it is begun, and Chapter 9 wraps things up.

■ WHY DID I WRITE THIS BOOK?

For the past 16 years, I have been honored to supervise a program in which skilled teachers and counselors assist struggling students in developing interpersonal competencies, emotional literacy, and academic success. In addition to this supervisory role, I have also provided staff development for teachers and other educators on issues affecting all students, including "at risk" students. As a result of this work, there have been numerous opportunities for me to note that many caring professionals struggle to remain positive and hopeful about students who seem to resist all efforts to engage them in learning and growing. These educators often feel overwhelmed and discouraged because they just cannot seem to reach their most challenging students, some of which are the brightest. They see potential being lost and it concerns them. Teachers and counselors ask for advice on what to do, what actions to take that might make a difference. I tell them that service-learning, when it is used appropriately, offers an option that often works when other strategies have not.

I decided to write this book to help teachers, and, in so doing, to help the students who may not be thriving in our educational system. Too many students go through school getting good grades but not developing the skills necessary for successful citizenship. Too many students drop out of school. Too many students who stay in school do not feel challenged, connected, or cared for. This book is for all teachers who want to make their course content more meaningful to all of their students. It is for teachers who know that they may not be engaging all of their students and who want to do something about that.

The examples of service-learning projects that are described in Chapters 6 and 7 are predominately geared toward a K–8 population, but they could be adapted to higher grade levels. While service-learning is a wonderful strategy for the hard-to-engage student, it is powerful for *all* students because it directly connects their course content to the real world, making what they learn in school meaningful and useful. Therefore, this book ought to be a helpful guide for all educators interested in connecting their students to learning through service.

■ WHY SERVICE-LEARNING?

In addition to producing graduates who go on to the world of work or higher education, the K–12 educational system ought to produce students who are competent and caring citizens. Service-learning engages students in learning about their communities, participating in active citizenship, and developing their personal social-emotional attributes.

I first observed the positive effects of service-learning when inner-city counselors in the program that I supervise began taking the most difficult, apparently unmotivated elementary students to a local nursing home to interact with the elderly. The transformation that took place within these students was remarkable. They began looking forward to school and participating more. The connection with the elderly, as well as with the caring adult who implemented the program, was magical. The students demonstrated that their behavior was totally under their control. Kids with problem behaviors in the classroom suddenly became polite, interested, and considerate. Their teachers reacted with amazement as the students who gave them the most trouble in the classroom transformed themselves at the community site.

WHEN IS IT BEST TO START SERVICE-LEARNING? ■

You may wonder why it is important that the elementary students I just described had the transformational experience of service-learning when it is high school kids who are dropping out. You might think that high school students need experiences like this more than elementary students do. The truth is that kids begin "dropping out" by disengaging from their learning early in their careers, some by fourth grade. Some may disengage because of boredom, others may disengage because of academic failure, and still others may disengage because they have little support from their families. By middle school it can be too late to engage students who are struggling academically and/or behaviorally. Students may wait to drop out until they are 16, but their dropout process begins long before that. Service-learning is appropriate for all ages, and although it is never too late to start, the sooner that it is included as an educational strategy the better.

WHAT MAKES SERVICE-LEARNING ■ GOOD INSTRUCTIONAL STRATEGY?

Service-learning encompasses all that we know about effective instruction and learning. The outcomes of service-learning, which would be difficult to attain through traditional classroom instruction, include students' creating meaning in and a relationship to the real world, engaging multiple intelligences and learning styles, and developing character traits that will accompany them into their adult lives. Offering students choices and opportunities to make decisions, encouraging students to work as members of teams, and allowing students alternative ways to demonstrate learning are sound educational practices, all of which are inherent in service-learning.

The most effective service-learning occurs when students are involved in the planning and implementation of the projects. Students who take part in making decisions and devising solutions for problems are engaged in higher-order thinking. When students have meaningful roles in ensuring the success of a project, their teachers are able to assume the roles of coaches, facilitators, and advocates. They create and provide opportunities for students, and then help facilitate students' working together to achieve their goals.

Service-learning was never meant to be the only means of instruction that a teacher utilizes. It is a teaching strategy that enhances subject matter, stimulates critical thinking, and promotes the personal development of students. It can make school better for good students, and it can make school better for marginal students.

This book provides sufficient background information and offers enough ideas for service projects for teachers to be able to adapt this amazing strategy to their own students' needs and interests. We look at various ways that service-learning is being implemented, and how it can engage students and inspire teachers. There are descriptions here of many activities that have been used as service-learning projects, and suggestions for teachers' incorporating them into their classroom instruction. Service-learning is not the only way to deliver curriculum and build personal competencies, but it is an effective one. I hope that this book will both inspire and convince you to do all in your power to begin incorporating this strategy, even in the simplest form. If you do, I believe that you will begin to see the kids before you as eager learners and resources just waiting to be tapped.

■ ACKNOWLEDGMENTS

I would like to acknowledge with sincere gratitude my colleagues who offered their service-learning projects, team-building experiences, and reflection activities as examples for others to follow:

Dot Beatty, Elaine Ormsbee, Elizabeth Miller, and Katy Sullivan-White, North Syracuse Central Schools, New York—Peer to Peer program

Janet Driscoll, St. Ann School, Diocese of Syracuse, New York—School Store Program, Broken Heart

Janet Fenner, Syracuse City School District, New York—I Care Kits, Goodness Gorillas

Catherine Kline, Syracuse City School District, New York—Freedom Garden, Dolls for Kids, African Museum, Senior Luncheons, Sharing Sack, Empathy Activity, Cooperative Monster Making, Broken Sentences, and What If

Lisa Murray and Chris Chandler, Chittenango Central Schools, New York—How Not To Fight program

Carol Norris, East Syracuse–Minoa Central Schools, New York—Nursing Home Visits

Elaine Ormsbee, North Syracuse Central Schools, New York—Helmet Safety

Judith Spaid, Fabius-Pompey Central Schools, New York—Clean-Up Day

Linda Spear, East Syracuse–Minoa Central Schools, New York—Mentoring/Tutoring Program

Valerie Stedman, Christian Brothers Academy, Syracuse, New York—Picture This

Carrie Zdobylak, East Syracuse–Minoa Central Schools, New York—course in service-learning

I would also like to gratefully acknowledge my special friends, Valerie Stedman, Sue Francesconi, and Lee Beals, who cheerfully took on the task of reading and editing my work to see if it all made sense! Your suggestions and insights were invaluable.

If it weren't for the brave counselors in the Alcohol/Drug Abuse Prevention Education Program (ADAPEP) who took the service-learning plunge, I would not have written this book. They made a believer out of me, and they have made school a better place for many hundreds of students.

Thanks to Rachel Livsey, Corwin Acquisitions Editor, for her belief in this book and for her encouragement when I wanted to give up on it.

Thanks always to my best friend and husband, Fred, and my boys, Dan and Patrick, who encourage me and inspire me daily.

I would like to thank the following reviewers of this book, whose critical comments were extremely helpful and are gratefully acknowledged:

Cynthia Parsons
Editorial Consultant, Book Author
Scottsdale, AZ

Amy E. White
Assistant Professor
University of North Carolina
Charlotte, NC

Neal Glasgow
Teacher
San Dieguito Academy High School
Encinitas, CA

Maria E. Stallions, PhD
Assistant Professor of Education
Executive Director for Outreach
Barry University
Miami Shores, FL

Paul Young
Principal
West After School Center
Lancaster, OH

About the Author

 **Kate Thomsen** is currently a consultant, facilitator, and presenter on a wide variety of topics related to positive youth development. She held the position of the Supervisor of Special Programs at Onondaga-Cortland-Madison BOCES in Syracuse, NY, for 16 years, where she supervised 40 school-based counselors. She holds a teaching certificate in English at the secondary level, a master's degree in Rehabilitation Counseling, and a Certificate of Advanced Study in Educational Administration.

Kate has a strong interest in the resiliency and asset development of youth, as well as in recent research on the adolescent brain. She has spent much of her career linking youth-serving agencies with schools in order to meet the needs of students at risk of academic or personal failure.

Kate has written one book, *Building Resilient Students: Integrating Resiliency Into Everything You Already Know and Do* (2002, Corwin Press), and the article "Positive Youth Development: If Schools Were Like Baseball Teams!" that appeared in the Summer 2004 issue of the journal *Reclaiming Children and Youth.*

1

The Power of Service-Learning

I hear and I forget. I see and I remember. I act and I understand.

—Chinese proverb

Service-learning is a form of education in which students learn academic content and skills by engaging in needed service in the real world (Boston, 1997). Service-learning has been on educators' minds for decades. In an article summarizing the then current thinking about school-based community service, Conrad and Hedin wrote in 1991, "Only time will tell whether the current interest among politicians and educators in strengthening the service ethic of our nation's youth will be sustained or whether new priorities or the same old pressures for higher test scores and improved basic skills will keep youth service on the fringes of the political and educational agenda. We hope that decisions about whether to make service a regular feature of school practice will be informed by evidence about its value to young people" (p. 744).

So, here we are in 2005, and service-learning is still not common practice in our schools. From a study of administrators, Scales and Roehlkepartain (2004) found that only 3 in 10 U.S. schools utilize service-learning. Seventy percent of the principals who do not provide service-learning indicated that the reason for this is that service-learning is *not required* by any standards that drive schools today. Middle and high school principals who are not incorporating service-learning also indicated that there is simply no room in the curriculum, and there are no resources available, for anything that is not seen as helping to comply with the No Child Left Behind act or raising testing scores. I believe that this book will help to change that perception.

Some teachers are having trouble just keeping up with the daily demands of the classroom. Some are confused about what constitutes service-learning, some doubt its effectiveness, some feel a lack of administrative support, and some feel a measure of trepidation about trying something new that may involve more work than traditional classroom teaching, at least initially. Clearly there is a need for evidence that service-learning is an instructional strategy that is effective in meeting standards and achieving good test scores.

This chapter will address these questions by discussing the origins of service-learning, its definition and prevalence, its benefits and positive effects, and the difference between community service and service-learning. But first, let's take an inside look at a class devoted entirely to service-learning.

■ A DAY IN A SERVICE-LEARNING CLASS

Recently, I encountered a former colleague who told me about a class she offers in service-learning. Now, as a longtime advocate for service-learning and a true believer in its benefits, I was intrigued. I immediately wondered how she was able to convince her principal and board of education to offer a class for an entire semester focused *only* on service for high school credit. Most of the *high school* service-learning that I was familiar with was part of a government class or a special project connected to course content. A class with service as its primary focus was new to me. She invited me to visit, and I accepted her invitation on the spot.

A Unique Experience

Shortly thereafter, on a warm, sunny fall day, I walked into a large high school, eager to meet with the students in her service-learning class. At first, the students who filtered into class did not seem very friendly. They sat quietly, eyeing me at the front of the room, not giving a hint of what was on their minds. I took a deep breath and started talking, hoping that something I said would elicit a smile or a nod. I said, "I am very interested in what all of you think about your experiences with this service-learning class. I want to know what difference it has made for you and what you have learned." I simply stopped talking and waited.

After a pause that seemed to go on forever, the students began talking and their words overwhelmed me. I began to see real people behind the once expressionless faces. Once again, I was reminded that I, like many educators, almost missed the experience of truly knowing these students. Because there are so few opportunities for students to make genuine contributions in their schools, educators are often deprived of seeing students as people who possess resources and talents that they are willing and eager to share.

The service-learning class I visited is unusual because most service-learning experiences are part of an established curriculum or are considered to be an extracurricular activity. This class, however, offers students the chance to earn .5 credits toward their graduation requirements through participation in service activities. I am sure this class is attractive to some students because of its nonacademic focus. The class engages students in service, but the service is not directly connected to the content in their other courses. Students focus entirely on the "other side" of service-learning—personal and social development. Of course, when they sign up, they are unaware of the transformation in themselves that is about to occur.

The class I observed was made up of 13 high school students, 10 females and 3 males, in tenth, eleventh, and twelfth grades. They engaged in a variety of activities: teaching third grade students about tobacco, assisting teachers in gym classes for special needs students, reading and role-playing with younger students, and assisting the elders at a local nursing home. They worked with special needs students within their own district and with regular education students at the elementary and junior high levels. On days when there was no service, they met to process and reflect on their experiences and to make plans for their next service experience. Their service was scheduled for every other day during the longer blocks of time.

The Students—Their Stories, Their Learning

One student told a story about "Joey," a special needs student who often acted out during class. She told how, while assisting in his classroom, she was able to get Joey to calm down and get to work when the teacher's attempts to do so had not been successful. She attributed her success to the fact that she and Joey had developed a relationship, and that he looked up to her and wanted her approval. That relationship, she concluded, was why he listened to her when she told him to stop his distracting behavior and get busy. This young woman clearly felt empowered by this positive experience, and she was able to make a powerful observation about human relationships that she will take into her adult life.

I then asked, "What would you like people to know about service-learning?" A young man said that he would like people to know that he and his classmates have made a really big impact on the kids and elders they work with, and that they are positive role models. He said that both the kids and the elders are eager to see them when they arrive and look forward to the days when the service class works with them. He observed that the kids and the elders seemed happier and more animated when the teens arrived.

Another student quickly added that the kids and elders that they worked with actually have had a big impact on them as well. She stressed that she feels happier on the days she does her service because working with kids lifts her mood. Other students concurred and spoke of having been in bad moods often and not feeling happy, but having had the experience of this class, feeling much happier in general. These students agree that service-learning changes you as a person. One student reported that she is more accepting of other people and is more able to control her anger because of her service-learning experience.

A student with special needs shared that when it was necessary to have a permission slip to go to the service sites, she never forgot that slip. Many other important things may still have been forgotten, but not that slip. There was no way she wanted to miss out on the opportunity to work with the younger students and elders. The regular education students reported never missing or skipping a day of school when it was a service day.

One student said that her grades had gone up because she realized that if she was telling younger kids to study hard and do their homework, then she ought to do it too. In fact, she reported that she made the high honor roll for the first time ever. Another student said that since she began teaching younger students about the dangers of smoking, she knew that she must never be seen smoking herself. She said she felt a responsibility to do what she said so that she wouldn't be hypocritical. Even though she sometimes smokes, she no longer does so in malls or other public places for fear that one of her students may see her. She has internalized a heightened sense of responsibility and awareness of role modeling that will serve her well in her adult life. The students reported to me that they feel they are righting the bad impressions that people often have of high school kids. They knew that their behavior was observed, and that they were giving teens a better name because of what they were doing.

Another benefit of this class, students said, was that they liked having experiences that they could talk about with their parents or the other adults in their lives. Their experiences gave them a starting point for conversation that offered them an opportunity to share what they had learned and to apply it to their own lives. They said that their parents were often surprised at the maturity of their statements and the abilities that they did not know their children were developing.

Students in this class have observed a big change in the teachers in the elementary school. They said that when they first started to go the junior high and elementary schools, teachers and other staff looked at them suspiciously. It was such an odd occurrence to see older students enter their buildings that elementary staffs immediately looked for the adult with the group to explain why they were in their school. Later, those same adults were excited to see them enter their buildings because they saw that they were having a positive impact on their students. They now trusted them.

By the end of this class, I was seeing these students with new eyes. They were no longer the aloof people who did not smile at a stranger. They were young adults learning lessons that will last a lifetime. They were kind, insightful people full of resources with dreams for their future. Two young men reported that they were considering becoming teachers after having had the opportunity to teach younger students. This class taught students lessons that will last a lifetime.

■ THE IMPACT OF SERVICE-LEARNING

The strategy of service-learning is like a vehicle that transports students to places they could only hope to go in a regular classroom experience. Through service-learning, and its integration of classroom work and service opportunities, students learn subject matter and develop personally. After having read the story of the service-learning class in this chapter, you may be wondering how arranging to have high school students perform particular services for others and then talk about their experiences could be so powerful. In this particular model of service-learning, the service performed was the focus. Their service was the vehicle that moved students toward increased self-awareness, self-confidence, and self-understanding. This service-learning class was designed for outcomes other than enhanced course content and increased academic achievement. The class was designed to connect students to school and to facilitate personal development. The teacher used service to others as the strategy to accomplish this. In other service-learning models, course content drives the service-learning, and social and personal development are ancillary.

The critical aspects of service-learning that help students develop personally and socially include connection to caring adults, cooperation among students, appreciation of one another's talents and areas of challenge, development of empathy, appreciation of different systems, awareness of personal competence, and application of knowledge to real-life situations. In a very real sense, service-learning often helps developing students to begin to answer the questions "Who am I ?" and "Where am I going?" After having had an opportunity to contribute their talents, students may find out what they can do and what they enjoy doing. Students, like the two young men who are considering becoming teachers, actually begin to picture themselves doing certain jobs and begin to envision ways to use their experiences in their futures.

Service-learning offers students opportunities to participate in meaningful ways. When students are asked to participate and to contribute their talents, there is an assumption made that they have talents. For some students, especially those who struggle academically, socially, and/or behaviorally, this is transformational. Offering students opportunities to contribute speaks volumes to them about how they are perceived. The offer to become involved in service communicates to them that they are capable, necessary, valued, and competent.

THE ORIGINS OF SERVICE-LEARNING ■ AS AN EDUCATIONAL STRATEGY

Service-learning began in the 1960s and went almost totally unnoticed until the 1980s when it began developing rapidly. It is both a practice and a philosophy of education, which began with John Dewey, one of our early-20th-century educational leaders. Dewey planted the seeds of service-learning through his philosophy of education and social reform. His ideas were later elaborated on by two educators, Kolb and Freire (Tai-Seale, 2000).

HOW IS SERVICE-LEARNING DEFINED? ■

Service-learning has been defined by many organizations. According to Billig (2000, p. 659), the Corporation for National Service defines it very comprehensively in this way:

A method whereby participants learn and develop through active participation in thoughtfully organized service that

- is conducted in and meets the needs of a community
- is coordinated with an elementary school, secondary school, institution of higher education, or community service program, and with the community

- helps foster civic responsibility
- is integrated into and enhances the (core) academic curriculum of the students, or the educational components of the community service program in which the participants are enrolled
- provides structured time for the students or participants to reflect on the service experience

■ THE PREVALENCE OF SERVICE-LEARNING

In 1999, a survey conducted by National Center for Educational Statistics (NCES) found that 32% of public schools organized service-learning as part of their curriculum (Westat, 1999). Researchers have discovered that many teachers all over the country are implementing service-learning in a variety of ways and, no doubt, with varying degrees of success. The 1999 survey provided the first reliable estimate of U.S. schools providing service-learning. This survey also tracked the type of support that is afforded teachers who are implementing service-learning projects. It found that 83% of teachers received support, but when the numbers are broken down, that support is not usually long term or systemic. Only 15% of teachers received extra planning time for service-learning activities, only 11% received a reduction in course load, and only 3% were hired as full-time service-learning coordinators (Westat, 1999). In spite of this lack of ongoing support, some teachers have adopted service-learning as one of their educational strategies. This may be because they see such positive results that they are willing to go the extra mile it takes to implement quality service-learning experiences for their students. It may also be that enlightened administrators encourage them to do so!

■ COMMUNITY SERVICE OR SERVICE-LEARNING?

Before we go much further, it is important to clear up the confusion between community service (volunteering) and service-learning. Many people continue to confuse these two activities that are actually quite different. In fact, community service has often borne the stigma of punishment. Many people equate community service with some type of reprimand that forces a person to provide hours of service as retribution for a wrongful act. Volunteering does not carry this same stigma, but rather, it is an optional activity that depends on the energy and good-will of those who engage in it. *Service-learning* is an educational term that describes an approach with the intended outcome of increased academic and personal learning. This learning is done through the connection of service to curriculum and students' structured reflection on the service experience. While community service and service-learning share the attribute of service to others, only service-learning consistently incorporates the elements of reflection and connection to curriculum.

Probably the most important aspect of service-learning is the time spent in reflection on the experience. Reflection can be done in myriad ways, depending on the desired outcome of the experience, the style of the learner, or the teacher's assignment. *Structured reflection* on the service experience differentiates service-learning from volunteering. It is when this reflection is done well that students' learning is deepened and critical thinking skills are honed.

There is value for students in volunteering, and there is even more value for them in service-learning. In a study comparing differences between community service and service-learning, Furco (2002) compared three groups of students. The study found that students who performed service to others developed more positive attitudes toward school, themselves, others, the future, and their communities. Those who performed no service at all did not acquire these positive benefits. Those who experienced meaningful service-learning activities in which they had responsible, adultlike roles were most positively affected by their experiences because these students felt empowered by the experience.

SERVICE FIRST OR LEARNING FIRST? ■

As Eyler and Giles (1999) wrote, "A lot of energy has been devoted to defining service-learning. In 1990 Jane Kendall wrote that there were 147 definitions in the literature, and there has been no falling away of interest in this endeavor since" (p. 3). In light of this dilemma, probably one of the most useful contributions to pinning down this strategy is summarized below:

Service-LEARNING	focus is primarily on learning goals and secondarily on service
SERVICE-learning	focus is on service primarily and learning secondarily
Service learning	service and learning goals are separate
SERVICE-LEARNING	focus is equally on service and learning, each enhancing the other

Source: Sigmon (1996).

This perspective is especially helpful for people who are struggling with the "right" way to do service-learning. If students are engaged in a service project, is it considered service-learning? The answer to that question lies in what else is happening in addition to the service. Is there structured reflection? Does the project have clear goals for the student and the project? Does the service meet a genuine need? Do students get involved in the planning and implementation of the service? Do they evaluate the project for effectiveness? Do students have an opportunity to demonstrate what they have learned from the experience? Is there a connection made between the service and the curriculum?

A service-learning class like the class described in this chapter is one way to implement the strategy. This class focused on *service,* and the learning took place when the students reflected on the experience. For the most part, learning centered on the students' personal development. There are also ways to utilize the strategy of service-learning that focus on *learning.* In the service-LEARNING approach, service activities are directly related to the subject matter in the curriculum. Students' learning is enhanced and deepened through the service activities, and their critical thinking and problem-solving skills are activated by the opportunity to apply their knowledge in practical ways. The service-learning approach chosen by a teacher depends on the outcomes he or she desires for students.

■ WHO BENEFITS FROM SERVICE-LEARNING?

No matter the form of service-learning, service and reflection can produce many desirable results: connection to school and learning through meaningful engagement of talents, personal and social skill development, and connection to caring adult role models and peers in school and community settings. These are desirable for all students, but for kids who are marginally connected to school, these potential outcomes can help to prevent their becoming dropouts.

The National Dropout Prevention Center at Clemson University stated that "service-learning is a teaching/learning method that connects meaningful community service experiences with academic learning, personal growth, civic responsibility, and preparation for the world of work. It can be a powerful vehicle for real school reform at all grade levels, K–12, as well as higher education" (Duckenfield & Wright, 1999, p. 1).

Service-learning is not only for difficult-to-engage students. All students benefit from connecting their learning to the real world. All students also benefit from increased connection with adults and with their communities. All students need to see that what they learn has meaning, and service-learning is one way to do this. For students who are thriving in school, service-learning enhances their school experiences and stimulates opportunities for advanced learning.

■ THE POSITIVE EFFECTS OF SERVICE-LEARNING

Service-learning has many benefits for students that entice teachers to implement this strategy in their teaching. Billig's (2000) compilation of research lists these positive effects of K–12 school-based service-learning:

1. Students who participate are less likely to engage in risky behaviors.

2. Service-learning has a positive effect on students' interpersonal development and ability to relate to culturally diverse groups.

3. Service-learning helps develop students' sense of civic responsibility and citizenship skills.

4. Service-learning helps students acquire academic skills and knowledge.

5. Students who participate in service-learning are more engaged with their studies and more motivated to learn.

6. Service-learning is associated with increased attendance.

7. Service-learning helps students become more realistic about careers.

8. Service-learning results in greater mutual respect between teachers and students.

9. Service-learning leads to more positive perceptions of school and youths on the part of community members. (p. 661)

FINAL WORDS ■

There is no prescription for service-learning, although the National Service-Learning Corporation, National Youth Leadership Council has defined Essential Elements of Effective Service-Learning Practice. These are presented in Chapter 3. All types of service-learning have value, from the simplest to the most involved. Educators, hopefully with the help of their students, are free to devise projects that meet their particular needs regarding subject content and community linkages. Some organizations, including the Maryland Student Service Alliance (www.mssa.sailorsite.net/ideas.html), have noted that service-learning projects fall along a continuum from direct service to indirect service to advocacy. Projects considered to be *direct service* involve students working face-to-face with people in the school or larger community, or actively engaged in an activity such as planting gardens. *Indirect service* projects involve students in efforts such as collecting food or toiletries for the needy. They often take place at the school site, and students channel resources to the needy rather than interacting directly with individuals needing the service. *Advocacy* entails students lending their voices and talents to draw attention to or help to eliminate the causes of a problem. Making speeches, writing letters, and making presentations are examples of advocacy.

Teachers all over the country are engaging students in helping activities in their schools and classrooms. As you read this book, think about how your students are already involved in active ways. Some schools have peer tutoring or peer mediation programs. Others have programs similar to Big Brothers/Big Sisters where older students buddy with younger ones to assist them in academic or social ways. These are wonderful activities that help to make schools exciting and caring places. As you will see in Chapter 3, moving from helping activities to service-learning does not have to be a daunting step. Before we get to that step, however, let's take a look in the next chapter at what the research says about effective service-learning.

2

Research
Into Practice

A person's true wealth is the good he or she does in the world.

—Mohammed

In the previous chapter, the benefits of service-learning were presented along with a brief history of service-learning. This chapter provides the research that supports the utilization of service-learning as an educational strategy. I elaborate on each research-based statement to assist you in making practical connections between it and your own educational circumstances. Later in the chapter, we explore the connection between service-learning and both character education and positive youth development. Once you have absorbed this foundational information, application of the research to practice will be much easier.

AND THE RESEARCH SAYS . . . ■

Educators who have been incorporating elements of service into their work with students already know what research on service-learning is now confirming—the positive benefits to students of this form of experiential learning are unmistakable. It is gratifying to see data that support intuition and observation. Shelley Billig (RMC, 2003), vice president of the RMC Research Corporation, has synthesized many reports and articles noting the positive effects of service-learning on students' academic, social, personal, and civic growth. The following statements describe the major benefits to students that Billig has identified:

- Service-learning is engaging students by incorporating strategies from research on effective instruction.
- Service-learning is helping students to improve academically.

- Service-learning is helping students improve their higher-order thinking skills.
- Service-learning is fostering young people's development of important personal and social skills.
- Service-learning is helping young people develop stronger ties to their schools, communities, and society.
- Service-learning is promoting students' exploration of various career pathways.
- Service-learning is creating more positive school climates.
- Service-learning is creating more community support for schools.

■ SERVICE-LEARNING IS ENGAGING STUDENTS BY INCORPORATING STRATEGIES FROM RESEARCH ON EFFECTIVE INSTRUCTION

Because service-learning actively engages students' participation and taps into their many different intelligences, it is a very effective strategy for engaging students and connecting them to school. Howard Gardner (1983, 1997) believes that there are at least eight intelligences. We know that schools focus for the most part on two, verbal and logical/mathematical. Students who are musically, spatially, kinesthetically, interpersonally, intrapersonally, or naturalistically intelligent excel in service-learning activities when their strengths are afforded opportunities to show themselves.

When students believe that what they are learning is meaningful, they engage in it naturally. This is one of the ways in which service-learning differs from instruction in traditional classrooms, where students have fewer opportunities to see the connection between what they are learning and how it is or can be useful in the real world. Whether service-learning is driven by *learning* (subject matter) or whether it is driven by *service* (personal or character development), service-learning is always connected to a need in the school or community that the students are working to fill. As a result, students immediately understand how what they are learning and what they are contributing is connected to the world in which they live.

Experts in instruction are beginning to understand how the brain learns. It is important for us to know that the brain of an adolescent is like a motion sensitive light; it switches off when no movement is noticed. Service-learning meets an adolescent brain's need for movement, variety, and novelty. Students who do not learn well through traditional methods may thrive in service-learning settings, because they have the opportunity to learn through a variety of modalities. For example, after having delivered meals to shut-ins, a student who had had difficulty writing essays would have much more emotional content to draw from and be more likely to write successfully.

Kinesthetic learners require movement and hands-on activities, and they learn content better when they are actively engaged. For example, if a service-learning project entailed creating a community garden, then starting seeds, digging, and planting are ways these students could learn about a science concept

Figure 2.1   The Learning Pyramid: Teaching Strategies and Their Retention Rates

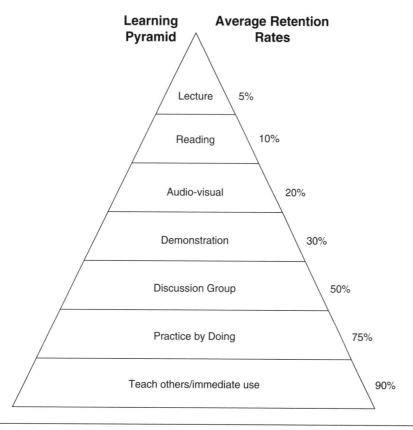

Source: Used with permission of Adams Center for Teaching Excellence, Abilence Christian University.

such as photosynthesis. Service-learning offers learning and instruction options to students (and teachers) that the traditional classroom may not.

Figure 2.1 is the Learning Pyramid showing the average retention rates associated with different teaching strategies. The source of these retention rates is research done by the National Training Laboratories (n.d.) in Bethel, Maine, which indicates that when students are active participants and immediately apply academic concepts in realistic settings, their learning and retention significantly increase. Sitting and listening to a lecture is the teaching strategy that resulted in the lowest retention rate. In practice, service-learning may integrate all of the teaching strategies on this pyramid, but because its focus is most heavily on the bottom half of the strategies, its positive impact on students' academic learning and retention is maximized.

SERVICE-LEARNING IS HELPING ■
STUDENTS IMPROVE ACADEMICALLY

This may be because students have opportunities to apply their newly acquired knowledge in a practical context, as we just saw in the learning pyramid. It is better for students to learn in complex contexts where they actively construct their own knowledge. Students rarely transfer knowledge learned in the class-room to new problems (Bransford, 1993).

To be effective, K–12 service-learning must be tied to state standards and learning objectives. Teachers may design projects that weave desired knowledge and skill building into the service experience, or they may design projects that weave service into the curriculum content. Students typically gain in the content area in which they are working because they have opportunities to delve into the material being taught and to dialogue on the material during reflection (RMC Research Corporation, 2003).

Students who serve other students through tutoring, role-playing, or classroom teaching may actually gain as much, or more, from the experience as those receiving instruction. Conrad and Hedin (1991) document strong evidence that studies of tutoring have found increases in reading and math performance for both tutors and tutees. An example of this is the high school student in the first chapter of this book, who after working with third graders to help them academically, began studying harder and improved her own grades. Later I will describe a program that successfully paired seventh grade tutors with elementary students. Students who teach are more engaged in their schools, are more responsible, and can see a connection between what they are learning and how it will be useful in the real world.

■ SERVICE-LEARNING IS HELPING STUDENTS IMPROVE THEIR HIGHER-ORDER THINKING SKILLS

Some researchers have found that many service-learning tasks help students to improve higher-order thinking skills. Analyzing, problem solving, decision making, resolving conflict, and communicating effectively are all skills that develop when students are exposed to meaningful projects where it is necessary to use these skills. Service-learning takes instruction and learning out of the typical classroom structure and into different contexts which may account for its power to facilitate cognitive development (Eyler & Giles, 1999).

Facilitating students' cognitive development sounds like quite a complicated undertaking, but it can be accomplished with even simple service projects. In a project described in greater detail in Chapter 5, you will read about fourth and fifth graders who visited a local nursing home to work with the seniors there. They played bingo and other games, and helped them move from one activity to the next. After visiting a number of times, their teacher assigned them a task to interview the seniors and find out what their school experiences were like when they were young. Many of the elders grew up in the same community and could tell stories about what life was like before certain roads and buildings were created. Students wrote about the information during reflection.

The experience of meeting and interviewing people who lived in another era triggered the students' imaginations and helped them to understand more fully what life was like in years gone by. Students imagined themselves living in the bygone era and wondered how they would have solved problems like boredom and transportation. What would they have done on a rainy day without TV or videos or computer games? How would they have gotten to school or a friend's house if their moms did not have cars to drive them in? Their imaginations coupled with real facts from a time long ago stimulated thoughts and ideas. History came alive for these students and they could see at the same time how drastically our society has changed in a relatively short period of time.

SERVICE-LEARNING IS FOSTERING ■ YOUNG PEOPLE'S DEVELOPMENT OF IMPORTANT PERSONAL AND SOCIAL SKILLS

Service-learning has been shown to have a favorable impact on students' personal growth in areas of self-esteem, self-understanding, sense of identity, independence, and autonomy. It also has had a positive impact on students' social development in the areas of interpersonal skills, cooperation, empathy, acceptance, and awareness of diverse cultures and peer group affiliation (Duckenfield & Swanson, 1992).

You will read in Chapter 5 about a project where fourth graders cut out patterns, sewed, stuffed, and decorated soft dolls for patients in the pediatric unit of a local hospital. As the students worked, they discussed what it must feel like to be in the hospital and how a soft doll will be comforting to a scared little child. Some students shared personal stories of their own hospitalizations or those of a loved one. As they cut and sewed, students talked about what they were doing and how the children would feel when they got a doll. Students developed empathy, received and gave support, came to understand the logistics of hospital stays, learned about why kids have to go to hospitals, and began to better understand the world in which they live. They also learned the practical skills of using patterns and sewing, and they had the satisfaction of creating something wonderful from pieces of material. Best of all, they had the satisfaction of giving their creation to someone else and getting a smile back as payment.

In addition to young people's developing character traits, like responsibility, honesty, reliability, and empathy, service-learning has other important benefits, such as helping them make connections to their peers and caring adults other than their parents. When I observed the service-learning group of seven students who were making the dolls for the hospitalized children, the teacher began by reminding students of the expectation that they would all be respectful and supportive during the time they were together. One little fourth grade boy raised his hand and said, "I want to try that out, ok?" The teacher, not exactly sure what was coming next, said, "Sure. What would you like to share?" The young boy went on to say that he was feeling sad lately because his grandfather had died and he wondered if anyone else had had that happen and, if so, what they did. I watched and listened as children offered their best thoughts to try to help. One girl said she goes into her room and cries when she is sad. Another assured him that crying will always make you feel better and he should go ahead and cry.

Kids who feel cared for by peers and adults in school will be more likely to stay in school and to do well. Knowing when and how to access support is a life skill that will carry over into adulthood if it is developed and nurtured by a young person. In order to learn well, students need to feel both physically and emotionally safe. This group offered safety to that youngster, and he was able to move forward with his day, a little better able to cope with his situation. This type of interaction is rare in a traditional classroom setting. Service-learning has the capacity to help students bond closer together and feel more positive about their school experiences.

■ SERVICE-LEARNING IS HELPING YOUNG PEOPLE DEVELOP STRONGER TIES TO THEIR SCHOOLS, COMMUNITIES, AND SOCIETY

Unfortunately, in the fast-paced world in which we live, young people are not always offered opportunities to positively engage with their communities. Research done by the Search Institute (n.d.) during school year 1999–2000, on over 217,000 sixth to twelfth graders, shows that only 25% of these students perceive that their communities value them. Only 28% reported that they believe that their communities view them as resources. Their perceptions may be accurate, but this reality can be changed through the vehicle of service-learning.

When students participate in service-learning, they automatically learn about their communities. Students learn about senior centers, nursery schools, dog pounds, soup kitchens, food pantries, and more. Too often these important community resources go unnoticed by young people, and even by some adults. Students gain an awareness of these sites and the crucial roles that they play in the functioning of a community. Adults who work in the agencies where service takes place gain the opportunity to meet young people and discover that they are willing and able to lend a hand. As a result, adult perceptions of young people change for the better. Likewise, students who make a contribution to their school develop feelings of responsibility and connection to their school and its faculty as well as their peers.

■ SERVICE-LEARNING IS PROMOTING STUDENTS' EXPLORATION OF VARIOUS CAREER PATHWAYS

Through service-learning experiences, students acquire skills that help them to make choices about possible career directions. They learn to be realistic about the world of work and what it takes to be professional. Important work values such as punctuality, consistency, attendance, honesty, and responsibility are learned in context rather than in isolated situations. They also meet contacts and gain references for job possibilities (Duckenfield & Swanson, 1992).

Students meet many different adults through their service-learning experiences. As a result, they get to see different ways of making a living that they may never have imagined. In addition to this important learning, students gain an awareness of their own capabilities. Service-learning offers opportunities for students to find out what interests them and what they are good at. In Chapter 1, we read about the class of students who are taking a course in service-learning. Two of the young men in that class are considering becoming teachers because they found out through their experiences with service-learning that they are good with kids and that they like being in the role of a teacher.

Students who interact with staff at nursing homes, hospitals, parks, soup kitchens, and other places where service-learning takes place have the opportunity to picture themselves doing these jobs. They begin to imagine themselves in roles other than students, and they begin to develop visions for their futures.

SERVICE-LEARNING IS CREATING ■ MORE POSITIVE SCHOOL CLIMATES

Research has shown that service-learning is associated with improvement in students, including more positive attitudes toward others and school, lower levels of alienation, and fewer disciplinary problems (Conrad & Hedin, 1991; Switzer, Simmons, Dew, Regalski, & Wang, 1995). That is what service-learning can do for students, but what about the teachers? Anyone familiar with schools knows that every school is unique, meaning that some schools feel positively energized and more inviting than others. Research indicates that schools that incorporate service-learning into their practices have teachers who are passionate and invigorated, and these same teachers provide more caring school climates (RMC Research Corporation, 2002). It stands to reason that if teachers are passionate and excited about their teaching, students will benefit from their enthusiasm. In addition, Billig and Conrad (1997) found that there was more dialogue about teaching and more respect among teachers and students in schools where service-learning was implemented.

Service-learning offers all students opportunities to shine through their own contributions. Students who are valued and recognized for what they can do, rather than what they cannot do, are less likely to be referred for discipline. Children do not usually enter the primary grades with the intention to disrupt or do poorly. Many children learn over time, as a direct result of their school experiences, to utilize those behaviors to cope. As Alan Mendler (2000) has said, "Most students who present themselves unfavorably, whether through their lack of motivation or their inappropriate behavior, are trying to conceal their concerns about academic or performance inadequacy" (p. 9). In other words, these students need desperately to feel capable. Teachers can help them do that.

As Michael Carrera, director of the Children's Aid Society, said, "Self-esteem is not taught, it is caught" (Carrera, 1999). This is done not by praising kids for what they do but by creating opportunities for youth to participate in activities, such as community service, that challenge them to develop skills and give them a sense of being valued for their work (Levine & Duckerman, 2004). Self-esteem is directly correlated with self-efficacy. Self-efficacy is the experience of really knowing what you can do because you have made considerable effort and have experienced some degree of success as a result of this effort. It is a belief in your own abilities and an inner pride that only comes when you have internalized your accomplishments. Self-efficacy is important for those of all ages.

In Chapter 7, there is a description of a service-learning project where middle school students in an afterschool peer leadership club visited a nursing home to work with the residents there. "Bobby," a child with a learning disability and attention difficulties, had been visiting with this group. In class, Bobby was difficult, but at the nursing home he was a kind, gentle, friendly person who showed no shyness with the elderly. He found going to the nursing home after school very rewarding. Many of the other students were initially put off by the appearance of the residents, but not Bobby. He bonded especially well with one person in particular.

One of his teachers, upon hearing of his work with this elderly person, was incredulous. She asked if she could go with the group the next time they visited the elderly, and the group adviser agreed. What she saw on that visit amazed her—the boy who gave her such a hard time in school turned into an angel when he was with the elderly people, especially his special friend. Why was that?

Bobby has a strength that he was not able to share in the school setting. However, his gentle and friendly nature and interpersonal skills were useful in the nursing home setting. In school, his inability to achieve academically thrust him into behaviors that were disruptive to the rest of the class and tried his teacher's patience. Without the opportunity to visit the nursing home, Bobby and his teacher might never have guessed that he had such compassion and desire to work with the elderly. His teacher observed a side of this child that she had never seen revealed in her classroom.

I had an opportunity to talk with this student, and I mentioned that many people work with the elderly and help them as part of their jobs. He said he did not know that, but when I suggested that maybe someday he might be able to do a job like that, he smiled and seemed to consider the idea. With the knowledge of Bobby's talent and interpersonal skills, teachers and counselors could build a plan to help this student succeed in school. The plan may include opportunities to mentor younger students, or assist teachers with routine tasks. The key is that people see Bobby for who he really is and what he can do.

■ SERVICE-LEARNING IS CREATING MORE COMMUNITY SUPPORT FOR SCHOOLS

In the small village of Fabius in New York, the ninth graders are given an opportunity to enter the larger community each year on "Clean-Up Day." Students rake leaves for seniors, set tombstones straight and weed the cemetery, wash the fire department's trucks, pick up litter, and generally work hard to make the village look refreshed. After only one experience with the kids, many of the citizens who were once wary of teens changed their attitudes for the better. Now, kids, even those who look a bit nontraditional, enter these citizens' yards and public spaces, excitedly chatting and eager to work. Once the citizens see the results of the students' labor, and when they take the time to say hello to the students, they find out that teens are not so scary after all. Clean-Up Day has become a yearly event that both students and community members eagerly anticipate.

This activity has benefited the school, the students, and the community. Seniors feel more positive about the students, and, as a result, they support the school during budget time. The students feel more accepted by adults in their community, and the community looks better overall, at least for one day in April! Activities such as this one can lay a solid foundation for more extensive service-learning connections within communities. As Superintendent Martin Swenson said, "Our mission statement, 'Enter to Learn. Leave to Serve,' was inscribed on the Fabius Elementary School building in 1931. Many of our senior citizens see this mission in the work our students perform, and our students learn the importance of serving others."

LESSONS FROM SERVICE-LEARNING ■

What is it about service to others that is so transformational for all concerned? Could it be transformational, for example, when kids go to senior centers and the elderly people greet them with smiles each time they visit and eagerly wait for them to talk about their lives? The students who visited the Hallmark Nursing Home in Minoa, New York, would say yes to that. One student said, "When we get there, they are sitting in their chairs with their heads down, but when they see us they look up and smile." Could it be that when they are serving others, kids focus on what they can do and never on what they cannot do? Seniors in a nursing home do not care what the report card says, they care what the child says. Could it be that, for kids who are having school troubles, the experience of serving is a way to build a positive self-concept and self-efficacy? As one student said, "I like going to the nursing home because it makes me feel good to help someone else."

Students have many resources and capacities for caring within them all the time, but traditional classroom experiences do not always bring out the best in our students. As one middle school student wrote, "I love being with someone who pays attention to only me. I wish I could go more often." Middle school students are very social and there is not much time for this in the traditional setting. A chance to socialize can be a great motivator.

SERVICE-LEARNING AND ■
OTHER EDUCATIONAL TRENDS

Character Education

The character education movement has direct links to service-learning. Interestingly, character education is not a new concept, just as we learned that service to others is not. Thomas Jefferson, just like John Dewey, believed that in order for our democracy to survive, people must have moral law within themselves (Lickona, 1991).

Since the 1990s, we have heard a great deal about Character Education. Our nation's emphasis on character development is in direct response to the changes in our overall societal structure. Young people today are growing up in a very different society than that of previous generations. Media influences have created a perception that young people are ready to do many adult activities long before they have the maturity to do so. Many important supports are missing from kids' lives and, as a result, many kids are floundering. According to the Search Institute (n.d.) survey done in 1999–2000, only 30% of students reported having positive communication with their families. Only 34% said that a parent is involved in their schooling, and only 30% reported having adult role models. The character education movement aims to fill the gaps that have developed as a result of the failures of adults to provide adequate structure, guidance, opportunities, and stability for their youth.

According to Thomas Lickona (1991), character is broken into three main areas: moral knowing, moral feeling, and moral action. It involves the head, the heart, and the hands. Children must know what to think about moral issues. They need to know the difference between right and wrong, to be able to see another's perspective, and to be able to make good decisions based on sound moral reasoning. On the heart level, they need to feel an obligation to do what is right. They need to be able to empathize with others' feelings and do the right thing even when it is hard to do. Finally, they need to have skills to turn moral judgment into action (Lickona, 1991).

Service-learning is a strategy that links the head, the heart, and the hands. Eyler and Giles (1999) talk about service-learning as a holistic approach that involves values as well as ideas. During reflection on the service-learning experience, students are often asked not only to reflect on the subject matter being studied but also to suggest what implications the learning has for action. Thus, the involvement of the student's head, heart, and hands that is required for character education is inherent in service-learning.

Many schools have adopted programs and initiatives designed to teach important values to our children. After serving at the nursing home, one fifth grade student wrote, "I learned how to be helpful to the seniors. I learned how to care about them." *Responsibility, empathy, respect,* and *trustworthiness* are words that are seen and heard throughout our schools. One of the most effective ways to instill these values is through service-learning. The act of service to others is character building in itself. The fifth grader mentioned above learned to be empathetic and to appreciate the differences between the seniors and younger people. Students learn to be responsible and respectful as they interact with those that they serve. They learn skills for social interaction and they learn about themselves. As one fourth grader reported, "I've learned that there is another person inside of me that shows I'm a leader." Character education is much more meaningful when it is tied to action in the real world. As an eleventh grader put it, "When you open yourself up, you learn about someone and that they really are not different from you."

Positive Youth Development

The basic tenets of positive youth development (connection, confidence, competence, compassion, and character) are inherent in good educational pedagogy, but many educators are unaware that what they do every day may actually be promoting positive youth development. If they knew, they might even be more deliberate about their efforts.

School-based positive youth development (PYD) challenges school personnel to think very differently about young people. In the positive youth development approach, youth are no longer "vessels" to be filled, "problems to be solved," "risks to be mitigated," or "subjects" to be tested. Rather, they are partners in their own development with voices to be heard. They are resources to be tapped rather than liabilities to be managed. They are people to be empowered rather than to be made compliant. Youth are perceived as future leaders, workers, parents, and neighbors. They are understood to be *in the process of becoming adults,* allowed to experiment with their ideas and to resolve any errors that might occur in the process. They are *hopeful* people who know that their voices matter, that they can depend upon caring adults to create safe environments where they will learn according to their unique styles, and that they will receive support and guidance when they need it (Thomsen, 2004, p. 80).

The link between service-learning and positive youth development is unmistakable. Karen Pittman, executive director of the Forum for Youth Investment, author, and youth advocate, writes extensively on youth development issues (see Pittman & Irby, 1996). She coined the phrase "problem-free is not fully prepared," which means that just because kids do not cause problems in school or at home, or are not plagued with obstacles to their development, does not mean that they are ready to assume a functioning place in society. In order to fully prepare youth for adulthood, we need to help them develop and hone personal life skills as well as academic skills. Giving youth a voice that matters in issues that affect them does this. Offering youth opportunities to contribute in meaningful ways does it. Connecting what youth are learning to the real world does it. What better way to accomplish these things than through service-learning?

FINAL WORDS ■

Service-learning is a powerful strategy for delivering curriculum, for connecting students to school, for building students' skills, increasing their academic achievement, and developing their personal character traits. It is a win-win experience for everyone involved. Service-learning is congruent with character development and positive youth development. It is not a new idea, but rather, has roots in the foundational philosophies of our earliest educational theorists. It is experiential learning that develops the heart and the mind, and teaches students how to engage in civic action.

The benefits of community-based and school-based service-learning are many. Communities feel more connected to their young people, young people feel valued by adults in their communities, students look forward to school, and teachers find that students learn content at a deeper and richer level.

Service-learning can be an important strategy if it is of high quality. There are guidelines to help practitioners develop high quality programs. In the next chapter, we will look at the Essential Elements of Effective Service-Learning to assist you in planning service-learning projects. You will begin to make conscious connections to the service-learning possibilities that exist within your schools, classrooms, and communities.

3

Turning Service Into Service-Learning

You must give some time to your fellow men. Even if it's a little thing, do something for others—something for which you get no pay but the privilege of doing it.

—Albert Schweitzer

There are thousands of teachers and counselors currently involved in service *projects.* They are working to engage their students in meaningful learning by connecting them to adults, peers, and their communities. They often do this without the benefit of a term to describe their actions or guidelines to guide their practice. In many cases, it would take a moderate effort to elevate their efforts to meet the higher standards of quality service-LEARNING.

Luckily, there are many researchers who inform the educational community about what constitutes high-quality service-learning. Melchior and Bailis (2002) found that the results from the Learn and Serve follow-up analysis indicate that one-time involvement in service-learning programs is unlikely to produce a long-term impact on young people. Researcher Peter Scales and his colleagues (Scales, Blyth, Berkas, & Kielsmeier, 2000) tell us that middle school students who regularly participate in meaningful and engaging opportunities to serve, and who reflect on those experiences with adult guidance, will receive greater benefit than those who serve on a project once or twice without time for quality reflection. While there are many ways to implement service-learning programs, there are essential elements that, when included, make some programs more effective than others. Practitioners need to know that there are important elements of service-learning that can enhance student outcomes. Scales and colleagues' study of middle school students involved in service-learning found that the differences between the groups were statistically significant when service-learning activities were sufficiently intense, when students found the service activities highly motivating, and when students were engaged in meaningful reflection on their experiences.

Differences in teacher creativity, parent involvement, type and duration of project, community acceptance, opportunities within the community, and level of student interest may account for why some service-learning experiences are of higher quality than others. How, then, is this strategy managed for quality? How do we know when a service-learning project is likely to be a valuable experience for the students? How do we know that we are providing the best service-learning experiences for our students?

Enter the Essential Elements of Effective Service-Learning. The National Service-Learning Cooperative has put forth eleven elements that serve to guide service-learning efforts. Teachers and other educators who are designing service-learning can refer to these essential elements as they plan their projects. The more of the elements that are present in a project, the more value the experience will have for students. These elements are listed in Figure 3.1.

■ SERVICE WITHOUT THE ELEMENTS

Many teachers and counselors in schools throughout the country are incorporating forms of service into their work with students on a daily basis. Some schools have clothing and food drives for the needy, and some collect food for animal shelters. Others ask that students perform some kind of volunteer work as a requirement for graduation. Some classes write letters to service men and women abroad. Others clean up streams and lakeshores or collect recyclables as a part of civics class. Peer tutoring within schools is not uncommon. Many schools are doing these projects without a clear understanding of service-learning and the research base that supports it.

For example, a school counselor told me about the MIND (Motivational Incentive for New Direction) program that she and her fellow school counselors offer for seventh grade students who have been retained. The program requires the students to give up one period per day of a "special" class, such as Home and Careers or Technology, in order to help out at the elementary school next door. These students assume various roles such as reading to younger students, tutoring, and occasionally helping teachers with tasks such as copying. The idea behind the program is to increase the seventh graders' confidence and self-efficacy, which had been adversely affected by their academic failure and subsequent retention.

Through this program, students have opportunities to connect with teachers in meaningful ways. They demonstrate their mastery of previously learned material by assisting younger students. Before long, the older students begin to see themselves as being capable of achieving success where before they only internalized their failures. Their counselor reported that they thrive on the fact that they are needed. In effect, they rebuild themselves through the act of helping others. As we will see, this program could be transformed into service-learning with the integration of the essential elements.

In another example, a special education teacher from an inner city school told me that she has occasionally asked "at risk" kids to assist her with her

Figure 3.1   Essential Elements of Effective Service-Learning Practice

Cluster I: Learning

Essential Element 1:   Effective service-learning establishes clear educational goals that require the application of concepts, content, and skills from the academic disciplines and involves students in the construction of their own knowledge.

Essential Element 2:   In effective service-learning, students are engaged in tasks that challenge and stretch them cognitively and developmentally.

Essential Element 3:   In effective service-learning, assessment is used as a way to enhance student learning as well as to document and evaluate how well students have met content and skills standards.

Cluster II: Service

Essential Element 4:   Students are engaged in service tasks that have clear goals, meet genuine needs in the school or community, and have significant consequences for themselves and others.

Essential Element 5:   Effective service-learning employs formative and summative evaluation in a systematic evaluation of the service effort and its outcomes.

Cluster III: Critical Components That Support Learning & Service

Essential Element 6:   Effective service-learning seeks to maximize student voice in selecting, designing, implementing, and evaluating the service project.

Essential Element 7:   Effective service-learning values diversity through its participants, its projects, and its outcomes.

Essential Element 8:   Effective service-learning promotes communication and interaction with the community and encourages partnerships and collaboration.

Essential Element 9:   Students are prepared for all aspects of their service work including a clear understanding of task and role, the skills and information required by the task, awareness of safety precautions, as well as knowledge about the sensitivity to the people with whom they will be working.

Essential Element 10: Student reflection takes place before, during, and after service, using multiple methods that encourage critical thinking, and is a central force in the design and fulfillment of curricular objectives.

Essential Element 11: Multiple methods are designed to acknowledge, celebrate, and further validate students' service work.

National Service-Learning Cooperative
National Youth Leadership Council

special needs students. In her school, it seemed that by third or fourth grade, the "at risk" students began to become disenfranchised. Their attitudes changed, and they began wearing gang colors and acting tough. As a way to engage these students in a positive activity, she offered some of them an opportunity to help her with her special needs students. They gladly accepted. She soon observed that this service had a transforming effect on the "at risk" kids. For very "at risk" students, being asked to help out is, indeed, a novel experience. Students who struggle with academics or behavior rarely are perceived by teachers as resources. When they are, the experience of helping another can often change them in positive ways that carry over into their own classrooms, resulting in better behavior or academic achievement.

The classroom teacher of these "at risk" students was surprised at the transformation that took place within them. While they were working with the special needs students, their behavior, attendance, and grades improved. This was in part because the "at risk" students had positive feelings about their work with the special needs students. This work gave them the opportunity to teach others what they know, to receive the approval of staff, and to take a break from the monotony of classroom work. Actively working with the special needs students addressed the "at risk" students' needs for movement and novelty. And without even knowing it, these students were developing empathy.

Everyone was a winner in this scenario. The special needs students loved the attention from the mainstream kids, and the "at risk" kids learned a better way of interacting with people. As it always seems to do, the opportunity to contribute allowed these students to show their better sides and allowed the teachers to see the potential that was underneath the tough exteriors.

Poor school behavior is often a symptom of two deeper problems that plague our students, namely, boredom and lack of connection. Perceptive teachers know that students like these have resources waiting to be tapped. Not surprisingly, the students described above rose to the tasks they were given. They embraced the opportunity to help, took their roles seriously, and began to show an improvement in attendance, completion of homework, and behavior. The power of service to others in reshaping students' behavior and, ultimately, their perception of themselves cannot be overstated (Conrad & Hedin, 1991).

Had the teachers fully understood service-learning and how to integrate the essential elements of effective service-learning into their work with students, the experiences that were offered to the students just mentioned would most likely have made an even greater impact. This will be the focus of the remainder of this chapter as we look at how service becomes service-*learning*.

■ MOVING FROM GOOD TO GREAT: IMPLEMENTING THE ESSENTIAL ELEMENTS OF EFFECTIVE SERVICE-LEARNING

The Essential Elements of Effective Service-Learning serve to guide development and implementation of service-learning experiences rather than to prescribe specific activities. Educators can refer to these elements to make sure that their activities have incorporated as many elements as possible. In practice, some of these elements may overlap. For example, Element 2 recommends stretching students both cognitively and developmentally, and Element 10 recommends student reflection that encourages critical thinking. These two elements certainly complement and reinforce one another. Research shows that high-quality, effective service-learning does not happen by accident. It takes careful, thoughtful planning by people who are clear on the goals they wish to accomplish through the service-learning experiences. Low-quality service-learning has little impact (Billig, 2004). Let's take a look at each of the Essential Elements as it applies to the projects described above, as well as to other common service projects.

Cluster I: Learning

Essential Element 1

This element has to do with incorporating educational goals, applying academic concepts and content, and involving students in the construction of their own knowledge. In the two projects that were mentioned previously—seventh grade retainees tutoring elementary students and "at risk" students working with special needs kids—there were positive things happening at four levels.

- First, the students who were performing the service were developing communication skills, interpersonal skills, self-efficacy, confidence, and empathy.
- Second, they were increasing their bonding to school.
- Third, they were strengthening their own knowledge and mastery of the topics being covered.
- Fourth, the students being tutored were gaining in knowledge and interpersonal skills and connection.

In these projects, the teachers could have made this service experience into service-learning if they had integrated Essential Element 1 by making the connections between the service and the curriculum explicit. The teachers could have provided opportunities for the serving students to connect their own tutoring experiences to writing (as part of structured reflection) or literature. The students could have read (or written) essays or fiction related to their experiences and then discussed them, comparing and contrasting their experiences with the information in the literature. The students could have been asked to teach newly learned information or skills to the younger students to solidify their new learning. The students could have written in journals about their experiences and the teacher could have read the journals and responded to them. These activities could have been considered for a grade. With the addition of Element 1, this good activity could have been on its way to being a great activity.

Those students who helped in the special education classes could have been assigned a research project by their own teacher. They might have been asked to discover the requirements for becoming a teacher or to research the positive effects of mentoring. They might have researched learning differences. Then, in addition to their personal development, their service would have enriched their knowledge, given them useful information related to possible careers, and satisfied a written assignment that could have been used for a grade. To be most effective, service-learning should never be a disconnected activity. Rather, it should be connected to personal and/or academic learning.

Connecting Service to Curriculum

There are many ways to connect service to curriculum. Take social studies, for example. Why stop at having students collect food for pantries when that activity could be coupled with learning about the causes and effects of hunger, poverty, or any type of economic issue? Why stop at having students write letters to Americans in the service overseas when students could learn so much more by extending that activity. Students could collect newspaper clippings about current events regarding overseas action, then ask the service personnel they correspond with about their opinions on issues related to the conflict—this would give them a perspective different from the ones in the news. They could further connect this service activity to their course content by reading literature related to war and discussing it relative to the current world situation. *All Quiet on the Western Front* comes to mind. Element 6 (student voice) could be integrated into this service-learning by asking students to design and implement a service project that would make a contribution to those serving in our armed forces.

When considering service-learning projects, teachers ought to review their curriculum and determine where opportunities for service exist. This will be discussed in greater detail in Chapter 4.

Essential Element 2

This element has to do with stretching students both cognitively and developmentally. This element was present in the example of the MIND program. The seventh graders who experienced the "failure" of being retained certainly were stretched when they went to the elementary school to read to and tutor younger students. It is difficult for students to change their self-perception and move from thinking of themselves as people who have "failed" to thinking of themselves as people who have something to offer. It really cannot be done easily without adult intervention and guidance. When asking students to take a risk that will stretch them, such as going to assist younger students, adult involvement is critical.

This particular program works well because the teachers involved know that the retained students need to experience feelings of self-efficacy and belonging, and they go out of their way to make this happen. Providing opportunities for retained seventh graders to read to or tutor younger students is not enough, however. If the seventh graders' experience is not a good one, their feelings of inadequacy may deepen. In this example, teachers take care to welcome the older students to the elementary school, to design activities for them that utilize their talents, and to monitor and adjust situations as the need arises. Ending the program with a celebration, in alignment with Essential Element 11, seals the experience and provides recognition for the risk-taking and effort that the students put forth.

Element 2 could be integrated into service projects such as letter writing and food collection. When these activities are done within the context of learning about a larger issue, they can easily promote the kind of critical thinking that stretches students cognitively. English and social studies are replete with opportunities to inspire students to delve deeper into their own thoughts and form important opinions about issues regarding poverty and injustice. Teachers could enhance the activity of collecting food and clothing for the needy by coupling this effort with assignments to do research and participate in guided discussions about the root causes of poverty and the personal and societal effects of individuals being raised in poverty.

- Students could apply math concepts to the activity, such as estimating the cost of food and how much food is needed for a certain number of people, the cost of feeding a family, the cost of clothing, and so on.
- Students could find out the average income of a family in their inner city, and then create a realistic budget to understand what poverty means.
- Students could visit to a shelter or a food pantry to deliver the collected goods, and this would assist students in making their learning real.
- Students could collect goods for HIV/AIDS agencies to distribute to infected people after doing research into methods of infection and prevention of infection.

Eyler and Giles (1999) wrote, "Service-learning programs that place students in contexts where their prejudices, previous experiences, and assumptions about the world are challenged may create the circumstances necessary for growth" (p. 17). When students are challenged to think about the task they are performing relative to the people who are being served, they begin to stretch and possibly alter their own perceptions of the world. Students learn that life is not as simple as it might have seemed, and that what is learned in books is only part of the story. The service-learning activity becomes a meaningful experience for students to reflect on through writing, discussion, art forms, and continued action. Students learn that real human beings with feelings just like their own appreciate their donations of food or their letters. Faceless people become real and students can understand how people might find themselves in need of help from others.

Essential Element 3

This element has to do with assessing student learning and determining how well students have met content and skills standards. In the example of the MIND program above, which is a SERVICE-learning model designed to improve personal and social skills, it is possible to assess students' attendance, level of participation, connection with their tutoring partner, and personal development. Some of these indicators are quantitative and some are qualitative, and this is always the case with service-learning. Teachers can track students' progress by reviewing records, observing behaviors, and collecting anecdotal and survey information from both the tutor and the one being tutored.

In other models of service-learning, such as service-LEARNING models where subject matter is enhanced and learning is deepened through service, assessment ought to determine how well students have learned academic material and acquired skills. Assessment can take various forms in addition to written tests, and it ought to offer students choices in demonstrating their learning. Experiential learning lends itself nicely to portfolios. Written reports, models, art, video, and even drama are ways that students might demonstrate their learning. It is important to provide students with rubrics so that they understand the teachers' expectations for their work. Service-learning that is closely connected to the material being covered in class tests ought to enhance students' achievement on those tests, since the students had an opportunity to connect their classroom learning to the real world.

The teachers whose projects are used here as examples could have elevated their assessment efforts by first determining what outcomes they were interested in accomplishing. Think about the service that the "at risk" students did with the special needs students, for example. If this had been a planned project rather than simply an inspired effort by a caring teacher to engage some difficult students, she might have given some thought to what, beyond occupying their time, she hoped would come of their participation in her classroom. Certainly she would have conferred with their classroom teacher to determine ways that they could work toward the same outcomes. If they aimed for improved behavior, grades, and so on, they might have considered what data they could look at to determine if any positive changes took place as a result of their involvement. For example, if they wanted there to be a reduction in referrals to the office, they could have found out how many referrals the students had prior to their involvement. If improved grades were the goal, then they could have gathered historical data such as completion of homework or report card grades. After working with the students for a period of time, they could then have compared the data to determine if improvement occurred.

Whatever data teachers collect to measure indicators of outcome achievement—completed homework assignments, office referrals, or attendance at school—it is important to be able to determine that the service-learning experience contributed to making the difference in the data. *In order to ensure this, it is necessary to know what the data are prior to service-learning and what the data are after service-learning.*

How can students' connection to school be measured? How can their motivation or change in attitude be measured? That is for the teachers who know the students best to determine. A student's arriving prepared for class or involvement in afterschool activities might be an indicator. A student's smiling or saying "good morning" might tell that student's teacher that an attitude change is occurring.

Subjective data, or the students' own perception of their learning, is also critical. Providing some way for students to let you know what they have learned is important in order to monitor and adjust the program, and so that you can communicate this information to key people like principals, parents, and other teachers. The pretest and posttest method can be very useful when determining the effectiveness of service-learning. The important thing to remember is that the pretest and posttest must have questions on them that are directly related to the outcomes you wish to achieve and to the service-learning experiences that the students will have.

For example, let's assume that you are implementing a SERVICE-learning project designed to build the connection to school in students in a middle school class who have been having trouble getting along. Your project design would incorporate the Essential Elements, and you would pay close attention to Elements 6 and 7, student voice and valuing diversity. Your assessment could be based on a pretest and posttest and could have questions such as these:

1. I feel that my classmates value my opinion.	Yes	No
2. I have many ideas that I would like to share.	Yes	No
3. Teachers seem to like me.	Yes	No
4. My classmates listen to my ideas.	Yes	No
5. I have respect for others' opinions.	Yes	No
6. I think my school is a caring place.	Yes	No
7. Service to others makes learning easier.	Yes	No
8. After serving on this project, I get along better with my classmates.	Yes	No
9. I learned a lot about myself during this experience.	Yes	No
10. I learned a lot about my classmates during this experience.	Yes	No

Of course, in order to have the desired impact, the SERVICE-learning experience would have to have activities designed to achieve the outcome of improved relationships and respect. Consider these:

- Initial team-building activities designed to enhance students' knowledge of and respect for each other's talents and diversity
- Having students work together on a service project that they design as a vehicle for learning and developing social and personal skills
- Giving students a voice in decision making, which communicates that you respect and care about them

It is important to remember that a SERVICE-learning experience such as the one just described will yield various types of learning for students because the affective and the cognitive really cannot be separated. If teachers carefully design activities and assignments that pique students' interests, stimulating their desire to know more about a topic, and also construct ways for students to develop respect for one another, then both students' learning and their personal development will be enhanced.

Cluster II: Service

Essential Element 4

This element ensures that service-learning has clear goals, meets genuine needs in the school or the community, and has significant consequences for students and others. Historically, Learn and Serve, Corporation for National and Community Service, saw service-learning as being conducted in and meeting the needs of an identified community (Learn and Serve, 1995). Much of the initial work in service-learning was done on college campuses where students entered the community to do internships and other forms of community service. As the concept of service-learning has made its way into K–12 education, the notion of community service has been adapted to better fit the unique needs of younger students. In addition to service in a community, service-learning also refers to making a significant contribution to a school community or even a classroom community.

The projects being used as our examples include this element in that the students were meeting genuine needs in the school community. The students who were doing the service knew that their work was important, largely because of the efforts of the adults in charge to communicate this to them. The special education teacher made sure the students understood that she really needed their help so that the special needs students could make progress. The elementary teachers who were part of the MIND program were waiting for the seventh graders with jobs for them to do when they arrived. All of the students who received tutoring benefited from the experience.

Had Essential Element 4 been more deliberately integrated into these experiences, the students would have understood what goals they were working toward personally and what goals they were working toward with those they were serving. The students would have had a clearer idea of what was expected of them. They would have been able to determine their own successes and analyze the areas they needed to focus on. Without a clear understanding of the goals and expectations for the project and for themselves, students' experiences may lack focus.

In all models of service-learning, having clear goals that students understand and accept as their own is very important. They need to believe that their work is necessary and appreciated in order for them to take it seriously and to believe that the community takes it seriously as well. Students need to believe that their efforts have made a difference for the people they served or the community project they have worked to complete. Offering students the opportunity to review the data from postsurveys done by those they served can be an effective way to convince students of the impact of their work.

Essential Element 5

This element encourages systematic formative and summative evaluations of the service effort and its outcomes. During a service-learning project, it is wise to periodically do a formative evaluation of the service activity that assesses how things are progressing. Changes in direction or focus are often necessary to ensure the project's success. Very often, plans are created in a school setting, but once students get to the community site, adjustments are necessary. Even in school settings, circumstances may change and adjustments to the project have to be made.

At the end of a project, it is key to summatively evaluate on three different levels:

- First, it is necessary to know what subject content students have learned or how students have changed (see Essential Element 3).
- Second, it is necessary to know the satisfaction level of the people or community served.
- Third, it is necessary to know which aspects of the project worked well and which did not.

The MIND program example was fairly simple to formatively assess for effectiveness. While there was no formal strategy used, the teachers in both the elementary school and the middle school kept in close communication. They were in agreement as to the goals of the program, and they could monitor and adjust their activities to ensure that all students were comfortable and were achieving the intended outcomes. There was no formative assessment built into the tutoring example used here.

If a service-learning project were connected with a community need, then the project coordinators would have to make the effort to assess the community's satisfaction with the progress of the intended service. Mid-project phone contact, visits, and surveys are all methods to determine stakeholder satisfaction. Since service-learning depends on schools being able to connect with willing community sources for projects, it is very important to maintain open lines of communication and to remain flexible so that everyone is satisfied.

At the end of a project, a summative evaluation must be done in order to determine if the project has been successful. Students' achievement and perceptions, as well as community site representatives' level of satisfaction, must be evaluated. These assessments can take the form of surveys and interviews. Community site representatives can be asked to fill out evaluation checklists on the students who worked with them, assessing the indicators that are connected to the goals of the project. See Figure 3.2 for an example of what this type of a summative evaluation form might look like. Remember, these forms must be customized and have questions and/or statements pertinent to the goals that the students were working toward through their service.

Cluster III: Critical Components That Support Learning and Service

Essential Element 6

This element has to do with maximizing student input into selecting, designing, implementing, and evaluating the service project. Students who understand the why of a project are full of ideas when it comes to how to accomplish the task. Just ask a group of kids how they could make their school safer, and they will offer some ideas. Or ask them how they could make the cafeteria a more attractive place to eat, how the school could make it easier for new kids to feel comfortable, how they could make friends with the neighbors who live next to the school playground. When offered a chance to solve a problem, kids are full of ideas. They need a caring, invested adult who will help them make their ideas happen.

Figure 3.2   Group Feedback Form for Service Site

The students from _____ school have worked at your site during their service-learning experience. Please give us your impressions of their work and conduct during that time period. Please assign a number from 1 to 5, with 5 being the highest grade they could achieve.

1. Students worked hard to complete their tasks. ___

2. Students were appropriate in their behavior. ___

3. Students interacted with adults in a polite, respectful manner. ___

4. Students showed improvement in skills as the experience progressed. ___

5. The quality of work that the students produced met my expectations. ___

6. This program fit nicely with our own routine and was not disruptive. ___

7. This program showed positive sides of students often missed by adults. ___

8. This program enhanced understanding between students and those served. ___

9. This program is a valuable asset to this organization. ___

10. This service site can offer even more opportunities for interaction between students and those who need to be served. ___

Please add any constructive critical comments that would assist us in making this program even more successful.

_____

_____

_____

Thank you for your time and willingness to partner in service-learning!

This same flow of ideas can also happen when kids are asked how to make their subject matter come alive with service. Teachers might present options for extended study through service. Offering students the opportunity to choose areas of interest helps to ensure their commitment to their learning. If a teacher said to a class, "We are about to study the effects of pollution on our environment. Can you think of any ways that we could help our community as we study this unit?" then I am willing to bet that the students would be able to think of some very creative things they could do. As these students moved through their unit of study, their projects would become more interesting and valuable.

According to Pittman and Irby (1996), there is nothing more important than offering young people the opportunity to be fully engaged in their own development toward becoming competent adults. Pittman and Irby believe that young people need to have a voice in the matters that affect them, but that involving students is not enough by itself. It is necessary to give them a voice that matters and supportive adult ears to listen to their ideas.

Any service experience must be meaningful to the students who are performing the service. The contribution they are making must be perceived by the students to be important and worthwhile. Giving students a voice in determining the type of service to be offered and the details of how to offer it is one way to ensure that they will perceive their work as meaningful. Another way is to help them to make connections through adult-led reflective activities highlighting the connection between what they do and how it improves another's circumstances (see Essential Element 10).

Essential Element 7

This element has to do with valuing diversity by ensuring that many different participants, projects, and outcomes are included in service-learning activities. Diversity relates to many more things than race. In addition to race, it can refer to diversity in learning styles, gender, socioeconomic status, culture, religion, and even taste in food! For many K–12 students, appreciation of diversity is difficult. After all, being like one another and belonging to a group is paramount for adolescents. They value connection, and one way to be connected is be like someone else. Many students who are different are ostracized by groups and made to feel less valued. Students are often assigned an identity by other students with or without their permission. Some of the more well-known labels that students have created for one another are *goth, preppy, punk, druggy, straight edge, jock, nerd,* and *computer geek.* Unless students have opportunities to experience one another as people with unique personalities and gifts, they will continue to apply such labels to each other. That is where service-learning can be quite helpful.

Teachers can not only design projects that expose students to issues and ideas that will open their eyes to things they never considered before, they can also design activities that reveal students to one another. In traditional classroom settings, often teachers do not get to really know their students, and students do not get to really know each other. Only when students have opportunities to work together and rely on one another do they begin to appreciate the unique contributions that each of them can bring to a task. Being able to understand and appreciate differences is a life skill that will continue to serve students long after graduation.

Essential Element 8

This element has to do with promoting communication and collaboration with the community. In Chapter 2, I described the Clean-Up Day in a small village where ninth graders enter the community and work in people's yards and public places cleaning up and beautifying the area. The program has done wonders for school-community relations, as well as for promoting understanding and acceptance between teens and elders. The school is quite satisfied with these results, but they could make this good program a great service-learning program with the addition of Essential Element 1.

If Element 1 and Element 8 were integrated into this service-learning project, this is what it might look like: Students might be asked to interview the senior citizens whose yards they were raking and cleaning up. Based on the intent of the interview, students could determine appropriate questions ahead of time and plan to spend a few minutes speaking with the seniors. The questions could be related to that day's activities, to current events, to health needs of the elderly, to the world of work, or to the history of the village. Health, career development, English and language arts, and social studies content areas offer teachers many possibilities for connecting this day of service to student learning.

Writing about their interviews and what they learned would make the Clean-Up Day experience much more academically meaningful to the students. Senior citizens would have the positive experience of being asked about their needs and for their opinions and recollections, which would solidify their relationships with the young people even further. It is even possible that students would be motivated to further civic action after hearing about the needs of the elderly.

Anyone interested in implementing this activity ought to consider giving the seniors the interview questions ahead of time so that they can prepare adequately. Seniors would benefit from the extra time to gather their thoughts, and the quality of the interviews would improve as a result of this preparation.

Essential Element 9

This element has to do with students' preparation for all parts of their service-learning, including their role, the task, the skills needed, safety issues, and knowledge about the people they will be serving. None of us would relish the thought of being thrown into an unfamiliar situation to sink or swim, and students are no different. They need to be prepared for their service experience in many important ways. When students understand why they are doing something, and how it makes a difference in an important and meaningful way, they are more apt to engage with the project and the process. The following list outlines what students need to know and understand.

- Students need to understand what they will be doing and why.
- Students need to understand the educational context that the service will be a part of.
- Students need to understand the situation they will be going into and what the people they will be meeting will be like.
- Students need to know what is expected of them and what skills they will be learning or practicing.
- Students need to know how to keep safe and how to keep those they serve safe.
- Students need a teacher or other trusted adult to forecast for them possible scenarios so that their expectations are realistic and their anxiety is lessened.

Team Building

Another part of preparation has to do with team building. This aspect of service-learning has been mentioned often in this discussion, and for good reason. If students are going to be expected to work as a group, they need time to learn about each other, to trust each other, and to appreciate the special talents each can bring to a situation. In the beginning of any group experience, team-building exercises are very important to help people warm up to one another and get comfortable working as group members. You can use the simple activity in Figure 3.3 below to get the team-building process started.

Figure 3.3   Student Partners' Interview Sheet

Interview your partner and put the answers to the questions in the boxes. Switch partners and repeat the interview. Then, introduce your partner to the rest of the class: This is _____ and this is what I learned about him or her.

Do you play a sport? Which one?	What is your favorite TV show?	What is your favorite video game?	What is the best movie you ever saw?	How many kids are in your family?
Do you have a pet?	Who is your favorite band or performer?	Have you ever broken a bone? Which one? How?	What do you do on Saturday?	Where were you born?
Would you ever get a tattoo?	Have you ever won anything?	What would your friends say about you?	What would your teacher say about you?	What is your favorite ride at the fair?
If you could go anywhere, where would you go?	What is the thing you are most proud of?	The last time you helped someone, what did you do?	What is your favorite sport to watch?	What is your favorite holiday?

Preparation of Adults

Another type of preparation that is extremely important is the preparation of the adults who will be working with the students at the service site. Any time students are brought into the community to do service, it is very important that the groundwork has been laid for their arrival and service participation. Community site staff members need to be briefed on the following issues:

- The intent of the program
- What to expect from students
- What they can do to make the students' experience most meaningful
- The goals and objectives of the service project
- How they can help the students to achieve the goals

Service-learning is a true partnership between the adults in two systems working together to provide the best learning experience for the youth who are participating. This understanding and true cooperation may take time to develop, but without it, students may feel at a loss for what to do and will miss out on an important connection with caring adults.

Essential Element 10

This element has to do with student reflection, which ought to take place before, during, and after the service to ensure that critical thinking takes place. A simple process lies at the root of Dewey's phases of reflective thinking—action-reflection-action. One way of focusing on this process is by asking, "What? So What? And Now What?" (Eyler, Giles, & Schmiede, 1996). It cannot be stressed enough that students' reflection on their experience is the key element of service-learning. Without the opportunity to reflect on experience, the learner loses the opportunity to make observations and explain them in light of new information. The service projects used here as examples lack the important element of structured reflection. Before their service, the students engaged in these projects needed an opportunity to think about what they were about to do, to forecast possible scenarios, and to anticipate skills that they might need to use. The students also needed an opportunity to process their actual experiences after service with a caring, engaged adult, in order to identify which of their actions were effective and which actions could have been improved.

Teachers in the MIND program noted improved confidence in the students and better attendance, but there was no structured reflection time during which they could share this with the students. The reason that having reflection led by an adult is so important is that many times students do not recognize their own talents and skills. A trusted adult often must point out students' abilities so that the students can see them. Sometimes great insights come when people talk or write about their experience and feelings. During group reflection it is not unusual for students to point out other students' strengths and abilities. This is a great contribution to students' connection to school and bonding to peers. Structured reflection is a time when both students and adults can discuss what was learned on a personal level as well as on a cognitive level.

Well-meaning teachers often provide opportunities for students to actively contribute in meaningful ways, but they may not recognize the importance of helping the students reflect on even the simplest activity. Teachers and counselors can ensure that their service-learning will be of high quality when their reflective activities are engaging and designed to deepen and solidify students' learning.

Essential Element 11

This element has to do with acknowledging, celebrating, and validating students' service work. This element varies in its implementation since some projects lend themselves to celebration more than others. Some projects, especially indirect ones, are less visible, and so celebration is unlikely unless the adults involved in the project make it a priority.

The special education teacher who utilized the innate good natures of the "at risk" students to help her with the special needs students could have integrated this element by involving the principal and the school community in recognizing the students' efforts and contributions. She knew of the great work the students did, the special needs students knew, but no one else was actively involved in recognizing the "at risk" students. Clearly, recognition would have increased the likelihood that these students would maintain their good behavior. It would also have broadcast to the rest of the faculty and staff, who often harbor less than positive feelings toward "at risk" students with bad behavior patterns, that these kids have a lot to offer if they are given a chance.

Celebrations of service-learning projects need to focus on students' learning and the contributions they have made. These celebrations are an opportunity for the community representatives to witness the amazing impact of their willingness to work with students. They are also opportunities for students to demonstrate for parents, teachers, and administrators what they have learned both academically and personally. Hopefully, the students will have been offered choices as to how they demonstrate their learning (in addition to traditional testing). Portfolio assessments are perfect for these celebrations.

SUPPORTING STAFF AS THEY ■ INTEGRATE THE ELEMENTS

In order to achieve high-quality service-learning, staff development is critical. It is unrealistic to expect that quality programs will be instituted or sustained without well-trained staff. In our fast-paced schools today, it may seem too time-consuming to spend time orienting and training staff in service-learning. On the surface it does not seem that complicated. However, service-learning is a multifaceted strategy, and ignoring the need for teacher and staff training is ultimately self-defeating. Every staff member who implements or even assists with service-learning must have a solid understanding of the goals of the project, for both the servers and the served. Staff must also have a grasp of the Essential Elements to ensure at the very least that service-learning includes preparation, implementation, and reflection.

Students are skilled at knowing when adults are going through the motions and when they are truly engaged and committed to something. Service-learning is too important to leave to chance. It needs passionate shepherds who will work to ensure that it is of the highest quality. Staff development is an integral part of forming a team of adults committed to service-learning.

The projects discussed previously were seriously in need of staff development and training. Staff would have benefited from an understanding of the Essential Elements of Effective Service-Learning Practice and from an understanding of positive youth development. They would have benefited from knowing the difference between service-learning and volunteering. Caring staff initiated these activities, but they had no formal orientation and training. If they had, there would have been connections made to the curriculum, structured reflection, and opportunities for the school to celebrate the achievements of the serving students. They would have understood that reflection and celebration are two elements that are integral to the service-learning experience. Offering staff development to these caring teachers and their administrators would ensure that their efforts to involve students in service-learning would be recognized and legitimized. It would move them to the next level and help to ensure that those wonderful ideas become institutionalized.

■ FINAL WORDS

Good service projects can become great service-learning projects when teachers and other staff understand how to incorporate the Essential Elements of Effective Service-Learning Practice into their work. To do this, they need quality staff development that will help them see how what they are already doing can become even better. It is unlikely that teachers will receive staff development unless school leaders endorse and fully support service-learning. This is necessary in order to ensure that it becomes embedded in the curriculum. Without school leaders' endorsement, service-learning efforts may be unrelated to the curriculum and haphazard, thus minimizing any effectiveness that could be expected from them.

Sincere efforts made by caring, dedicated teachers may not be sustained, leading to the discouragement of both teachers and students. With strong leadership that includes allotment of resources, service-learning can be the strategy that engages the disengaged, motivates the motivated students to delve deeper, and energizes teachers and staff. (For more about sustaining service-learning efforts, see Chapter 8.)

In Chapter 4 we take a look at the activities that are necessary in preparing to design and implement service-learning projects. Preparation is very important, as only through planning can you ensure that your service-learning projects have the intended impact on students' learning and personal development.

4

Laying the Groundwork for Service-Learning

Unless we think of others and do something for them, we miss one of the greatest sources of happiness.

—Ray Lyman Wilbur

As Stephen Covey said in his book *The 7 Habits of Highly Effective People* (1990), "begin with the end in mind." This means let your intended outcomes lead your way. Know where you want to go, and then design your activities to get you there. It is important to remember this when starting a service-learning project. And, to reference a cliché, never bite off more than you can chew.

When considering a service-learning project, it is best to start by establishing the focus of your project. Will your project be SERVICE-learning, where the primary goal is to provide service from which students gain broad benefits such as self-confidence, interpersonal skills, social responsibility, citizenship, and connection to school? Or will your project be service-LEARNING, where your primary goal is to enhance curriculum content through service? Subject content directs the activities of a service-LEARNING approach, while a SERVICE-learning approach has almost limitless possibilities for projects.

In Chapter 1, I outlined the three levels of service-learning—direct service, indirect service, and advocacy—and the activities associated with each level. *Direct service* requires the most intense preparation and implementation because it usually involves traveling to service sites or, if service is to be done within the school, adjusting and coordinating schedules. Traveling with students means procuring permission slips, scheduling to avoid conflicts, and doing the many other tasks necessary to prepare for entry into the community. *Indirect service* requires less preparation and action because very often students can perform their service at the school, and the fruits of their labor can be delivered, mailed, or somehow sent to the people or site being served. *Advocacy* requires the least logistical preparation since this type of service generally requires action such as letter writing, research, and/or making presentations. All three levels of service are important, and the level that is best suited to your project ought to be chosen based on criteria such as these:

- Whether your primary goal is curricular enhancement or students' personal development
- The time available for service
- The availability of community linkages
- Your transportation requirements
- The abilities and interests of the students

The following sections contain important suggestions to consider when implementing service-learning for the first time.

■ WHEN IN DOUBT, START SMALL

Any time you do something for the first time, there is a learning curve. It is impossible to anticipate all of the problems and issues beforehand; therefore, it is important to be sure that first-time projects are doable. If they become too cumbersome, it is easy to get discouraged quickly and give up too soon. Kids love the hands-on aspect of service-learning, and it is very damaging to students to start something and then have to abandon it because you were not adequately prepared when you began.

It is often advisable to try indirect service-learning initially as a way to build contacts and relationships within the community. The yellow pages of the phone book are a great place to look for service-learning opportunities. Make a list of agencies or human service organizations in proximity to your school, and as you browse the pages, think of aspects of your curriculum that could be connected to the community. Figure 4.1 offers some ideas for projects.

Keeping a list of agencies and programs with names of contact people really helps as you begin to incorporate service projects into your repertoire. Summer is a great time to make visits and introduce yourself to people who may have an interest in working with the students, either directly or indirectly.

Once you have decided what your primary goals are, you can introduce the idea to the students. If your primary goal is to connect service to a facet of your curriculum, then your students will need to know what it is they will be learning and how the service is connected to it. Since you have already spent time making community contacts and developing relationships with interested agencies, the next step is to introduce your students to the community site possibilities. Very often, representatives from agencies or service sites will agree to come to talk to students to tell them about their programs and to explain ways that the students can help.

Figure 4.1   Service-Learning Activities

---

25 Ideas for Service-Learning Activities

1. **Animal shelters:** collecting food, money, walking animals, cleaning cages, collecting old blankets for beds

2. **Food pantries:** collecting food, sorting food, disseminating food, cleaning pantries

3. **Growing food for pantries:** students plant and grow vegetables that will be donated to food pantries

4. **Beautification projects:** students plant gardens, clean up areas, adopt parks or playgrounds to keep clean

5. **American Cancer Society:** collecting money, making awareness presentations, making cards for patients undergoing chemotherapy, visiting with those undergoing treatment

6. **Juvenile Diabetes Foundation, Cystic Fibrosis Foundation, etc.:** collecting money, making awareness presentations, reaching out to kids afflicted with the disease

7. **Nursing homes:** helping patients move from one place to another, playing games, visiting, joining for a meal, bringing cards, interviewing residents, visiting at the holidays

8. **Senior citizen centers:** playing games, interviewing seniors, serving meals, visiting

9. **Local parks and recreation offices:** clean-up crews, create pooper scooper awareness posters

10. **Alzheimer's units:** visiting with patients, bringing music and cards

11. **Local hospitals:** making cards and/or dolls for sick kids, collecting blankets or other goods for new babies in need

12. **American Red Cross:** publicizing blood drives, helping with disaster needs

13. **UNICEF:** organizing a collection for UNICEF at Halloween and other times

14. **Nature centers:** clean-up crews, testing water, collecting specimens and samples of flora

15. **Salvation Army:** clothing, food collection; donation of books for homeless shelters, pen pals with kids in shelters

16. **Centers for the blind:** recording books on tape

17. **Daycare centers:** recording children's books for kids to listen to

18. **Voter registration:** writing letters to encourage people to vote, assisting on election day

19. **Local churches:** help elderly parishioners with shopping, yard work, snow shoveling, and visiting the lonely

20. **Local department of health and safety:** make awareness presentations regarding health and safety issues for kids such as bicycle helmets, padding for skaters, nutrition, drug use, stranger danger, etc.

21. **Fire departments:** make presentations to younger kids about fire safety, create posters, write and perform plays for younger students

22. **Police departments:** work with police to learn about issues related to driving, safety, etc. and then teach younger students, create awareness posters, etc.; have younger students write to older students asking them to be careful at prom time

23. **Alcohol councils:** students research drug and alcohol abuse issues and make presentations (visual, art, music, drama) to younger students and/or parents

24. **Grocery bag messages:** students get unused paper grocery bags from the local supermarket and write messages on them. Students could research any number of topics such as staying healthy, eating healthy, drinking and driving, drug abuse, child development, parenting strategies. They then write bullets of information on the bags so customers will see them when they buy groceries.

25. **Aid for our armed services:** students can write letters, collect donations, fill and send goodie bags, make cards, conduct interviews. Students can develop ongoing correspondence with one or more service personnel. They can write stories about the information they receive, write reports about service life, draw maps of the places where the people are stationed, study the natural features of the places where the people are stationed, etc. At the same time, they will brighten the day of a service person and help to keep them connected to home.

■ SEARCH YOUR CURRICULUM FOR OPPORTUNITIES

The service ideas above would, of course, need to be connected to the curriculum in order to become service-learning. Luckily, there are service opportunities inherent in almost all subjects. Teachers just have to seek out the connections. English and language arts are especially easy to connect to service opportunities. Literature about animals, such as the classic *Black Beauty*, could be one of the curricular connections to collecting for animal shelters. There are many other newer animal-related novels at all reading levels that teachers could integrate into their literature choices.

Stories about Helen Keller could be connected to students' making tapes for the blind. Students would learn about this influential person in American history, and at the same time develop an understanding of the challenges facing people with limited or no vision.

Students could learn about the work of UNICEF as part of global studies, and then their service of money collection would be more meaningful. The content of health classes on diseases like cancer could be linked to the sale of daffodils, and certainly math could be connected to the project by asking students to make change and to calculate a feasible monetary goal based on the number of staff and students in their building. The possibilities are endless. Students doing advocacy can write letters, reports, and essays and make presentations on particular topics that they are interested in teaching others more about (such as pollution, asthma, environmental protection, etc.).

Social studies and science lend themselves nicely to direct and indirect forms of service-learning. The citizenship aspect of social studies is a perfect place for students to connect service to learning. They can get involved in political issues and advocate for causes they believe in. They can learn about the right to vote, and they can work to remind people to vote during election time. Planting community gardens, cleaning up streams, and protecting ecosystems relate to both citizenship and science topics. These subjects come alive when concepts are applied in real-world settings. Whenever students are involved in planning and decision making there are sure to be opportunities to apply principles of mathematics. Estimating, measuring, and calculating all make more sense when they can be applied to a hands-on project.

■ TEAM WITH OTHER TEACHERS AND CONSIDER THE BIG PICTURE

In the best of circumstances, all teachers on a team would confer regarding how they might offer students opportunities to serve that would connect to more than one subject area. In many schools, social studies and English and language arts are closely aligned so that one project could relate to both areas of study. The same is true for science and math. Teachers need to collaborate in order to find ways for students to learn by serving. The initial investment of time would be worthwhile, as students really begin to see the connections between their different subjects as well as the connection between their learning and the real world.

Giving students voice and choice in their service-learning is essential. Most adults who attend important meetings expect to know what is on the agenda. Why should students be left in the dark? It would be helpful for students if their teachers provided a big-picture view of the content to be studied during a course. If the students knew the course content ahead of time, they might like to select an area that they would like to connect to a service project.

For example, if students know that in science they will be studying ecosystems at some point during the year, maybe they would choose to do a service-learning project related to water pollution or recycling. Maybe their English teacher would assign literature or nonfiction related to the same topic, and maybe their math teacher could devise assignments that would help them put related math skills and concepts into action. Estimating how much money could be saved through recycling and how many trees it takes to create a ream of paper might be interesting assignments. With a little effort and communication, teachers, with their students, could turn these "maybes" into actualities. Students then would be more invested in their learning because they had a voice in their choices.

MAKE SURE THERE IS ENOUGH TIME ■

Time is critical to the success of a service-learning project because learning takes time. The research is very clear that students derive the most benefit from service-learning when there is enough time spent in service and reflection (Scales et al., 2000). Students need time to do research related to assignments, and/or to acquire some degree of competence in their service activities. Intensity and duration of students' efforts are critical if service-learning is to have an impact on students' learning and personal development. When students spend enough time with those they serve, relationships develop that form the basis for positive personal changes. Through such relationships, students develop responsibility, respect, self-confidence, and academic skills. This takes time, and students cannot be expected to develop these attributes when service is done only once or twice.

If students are going to be working together in service-learning projects, they need to know and trust one another. It is therefore wise to involve students in team-building activities prior to their performing service as a team. (See Chapter 5 for more on this.)

LINE UP YOUR TACTICAL RESOURCES FIRST ■

Some service activities, especially those that involve direct service, require transportation and other resources. It is important that whoever is coordinating the service-learning project lays out a plan for provision of necessary resources before involving students in the project. The plan may need to include the actions outlined below.

Enlist Support From Others

Consider using parent club volunteers for tasks that are time-consuming or need to be done during teaching hours. Parents are often very willing to do much more than bake cookies, but they are often not asked. Choose one or two dependable, creative parents and make them your partners. Meet with them to share the goals of the project and to help them understand what service-learning is. They will become invested in the strategy and work to help you be successful for the sakes of their children. They can make phone calls to agencies, solicit donations, and call other parents to enlist their support.

If you are taking students off school grounds, it is important to have enough chaperones to ensure safety. Teachers that are cooperating with you on a service-learning project would be logical to enlist. Calling on parents or other school staff may also be necessary. Even if the project does not involve transporting students, parents can often be lifesavers because they will help monitor students, assist them with tasks, and provide refreshments. Here is an example of a parent enlistment letter:

Dear _____,

My fifth grade class at _____ school is going to be studying about pollution. As a service-learning project, we are going to be collecting paper and cans for recycling. We have many activities planned for both in school and in the community. Our goal is to emphasize the importance of recycling by creating a visual image of the amount of paper and cans consumed in one month. If you could help us in any of the following ways, please check the box and return this form to me. (I will be in touch very soon.)

☐ I can chaperone students at their Saturday can and paper collection site on the circled dates: March 10, March 17, March 24, March 31.

☐ I can help bring collected paper and cans to the recycling center when the project is over.

☐ I can bake cookies for the days of collection.

☐ I can donate large bags for can collection.

☐ I can save my recyclable paper from home and have my child bring it to school.

☐ I can make sure my child gets to the library to do research on pollution.

Thank you for all of your help,

Set Up Transportation

Make sure transportation is available for specific activities. Service-learning is usually very cost-effective, except when it is necessary to pay for transportation. If your school district will not or cannot provide busing for students to and from sites, it may be necessary to raise funds to pay for transportation. Arranging for busing, even if it is free, can be time-consuming, so you need to figure that logistic into your service-learning project. If transportation is provided by parents or other volunteers, be sure to check with your district's policy on insurance coverage to make sure the drivers are covered. Also, never forget to get permission from parents for their students to ride in a car with another adult.

Transportation can be an issue when planning for direct service projects. It can be easier with older students than with younger ones, since they can often get themselves to service sites after school hours or on weekends and do not need to rely on the school for transportation. Parents are often willing to transport their younger children to sites. If, however, transportation is difficult for some students and they cannot do direct service without it, there are many ways that they can serve within the school setting by organizing drives or doing advocacy work related to the topic they have chosen.

Communicate With the Community

This is initially time-consuming, but it is necessary to develop projects and enlist support from other caring adults. (That is why we start small!) Organizations will want to know what you expect of them as well as what you will offer them. Sometimes it may seem like a bother to bring in groups of people to help in some way. After all, it takes time to orient new helpers and communicate your wishes and level of expectation to them. Some senior centers will enjoy having students come to help serve lunches or assist with games during the day, but they do not want to have to develop a program for working with the students. When initiating contact, it is a good idea to alleviate fears that the agencies will have to be responsible for the students. If you make it known that the students are there to serve them, they will be more receptive to opening their doors. Ask the supervisor to identify some needs that their organization has so that you might determine if your students could help provide what they need.

It is wise to be very clear with community organizations. Tell them that you will provide supervision and monitor outcomes, so they will not have responsibility for the students, but they will have the responsibility for understanding the goals of the service-learning project and for doing their part to help students to achieve those goals.

Ensure That There Are Adequate Supplies

Here is an example of a very simple gesture that takes planning, which is the only way to ensure that there will be enough supplies for all the students. A teacher told me about a service-learning project that centers on delivering Meals on Wheels to people who are housebound. One of the preliminary activities that she has the students do is to make greeting cards for the people receiving the meals. As the students work, they imagine the kinds of things that would cheer people up and try to communicate those things through their cards. The cards are then presented to the people with their meals. It is a way of personalizing the delivery and of making the people real to the students. Of course, the cards are much appreciated by the housebound people, some of whom may be very lonely. Even simple activities like this one require the teachers' planning ahead.

Make Sure There Are Jobs for All Students

Make sure that all students have a job to do. Recently I spoke with a teacher and a counselor who are planning to do a service-learning project that will involve starting seedlings and then planting a flower garden. As they talked about their idea, they began to strategize ways to keep all the students engaged in the project. When teachers do a long-term project, it is sometimes a challenge to maintain students' interest and involvement. In this case, the teachers will need to keep the students engaged while they wait for the seeds to grow, so they decided to have the students work on committees such as the fundraising committee, the communications committee, and the garden design committee. All the students will participate in planting the seeds, but while the seeds germinate and grow, the students will be actively engaged in the project through their committees. The teachers decided to connect the project to academic skills through the students' activities, such as writing letters to businesses to ask for donations, doing publicity to schoolmates and parents about the garden, developing a budget, and computing costs. The teachers thought it would also be a good idea to plan a field trip to local gardens to give the students the opportunity to get ideas for how to design their garden.

Teachers must plan in advance how they will keep students actively engaged in the project, and using student committees is one great way to do this. When teachers form student committees, they become committee facilitators and support student ideas, giving students ownership of and a voice in the project.

Create and Monitor Completion of Permission Slips

Make sure that permission slips are created, approved, and signed. Every school has its own policy on travel and participation in field trips. Service-learning is very similar to a field trip, and some schools just use the same form for both. Permission forms should have enough information on them to communicate effectively to parents the nature of the activity and its time frame, as well as to anticipate any concerns parents might have (such as whether it will interrupt their normal routine in any way). Because these slips are so important when students will be leaving the school premises, it is wise to get them signed right away. Sometimes these slips get lost in backpacks and never make it home, so be prepared to have extras on hand. Start collecting them a week or so in advance so that forgetful students do not miss out on the chance to participate. An example of a permission form follows.

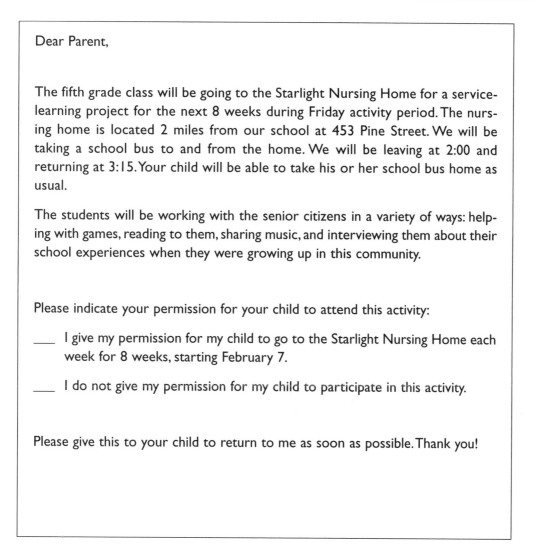

Dear Parent,

The fifth grade class will be going to the Starlight Nursing Home for a service-learning project for the next 8 weeks during Friday activity period. The nursing home is located 2 miles from our school at 453 Pine Street. We will be taking a school bus to and from the home. We will be leaving at 2:00 and returning at 3:15. Your child will be able to take his or her school bus home as usual.

The students will be working with the senior citizens in a variety of ways: helping with games, reading to them, sharing music, and interviewing them about their school experiences when they were growing up in this community.

Please indicate your permission for your child to attend this activity:

____ I give my permission for my child to go to the Starlight Nursing Home each week for 8 weeks, starting February 7.

____ I do not give my permission for my child to participate in this activity.

Please give this to your child to return to me as soon as possible. Thank you!

Procure the Necessary Funds

Decide whether a particular activity requires money, and apply for the necessary funds and/or consider fundraising. Service-learning does not have to be very costly, but there are expenses to consider. Sometimes students can be part of the solution to the problem of more expenses than funds by actively raising the money or requesting the supplies needed for their service-learning project. For example, students can write letters to companies asking for donations of seeds, soil, pots, and tools in preparation for a garden project. Students can also have bake sales, have car washes, or rent themselves out for a day to younger students to raise money for service-learning projects. In fact, the activity of fundraising is educational in itself when students have the opportunity to estimate the amount of money needed for a project, create a budget, and then actually raise money using computational skills like making change.

Supplies for certain activities and celebrations are expenses associated with service-learning projects. And, as already mentioned, busing costs can be an obstacle. As teachers develop and plan for their projects, it is critical for them to consider how much money they will need. Very often parent clubs can help out with expenses. Another possibility is the use of Title IV funds because service-learning is considered to be a best practice in the creation of safe and drug-free schools.

■ INVITE STUDENTS TO TELL THEIR STORIES

Students' voices are powerful. School boards of education, administrators, parents, and community members are often very moved when students communicate directly with them. Once service-learning projects are complete, participants can develop presentations describing the benefits of their activities. Hearing directly from students that service-learning has enhanced their learning and has helped them to develop in positive ways may help to convince reluctant supporters that this is a worthwhile endeavor.

Some counselors conduct service-learning as part of their programs designed to reach "at risk" students. It is very important for these students to be given the opportunity to present their learning, both personal and academic, to their classroom teachers and parents. Teachers and parents may not have had an opportunity to see these students in a positive light before. Students often totally amaze their classroom teachers when they are given opportunities to learn and serve outside of the traditional classroom setting. Students need not only a voice in planning and implementing service-learning but also the opportunity to demonstrate their growth.

■ FINAL WORDS

Planning and preparation are second nature to teachers, and that is a good thing because service-learning takes careful thought and preparation. Starting with the end in mind is important because it ensures that teachers will plan and implement service-learning activities that will support the desired outcomes.

Service-learning is initially time-consuming when teachers are working to develop community connections and relationships with potential service sites. Any first-time effort entails more work, but that work lessens as contacts are established and projects are completed. Recruiting helpful and committed parents can lighten the load considerably, especially when parents become partners in service-learning.

Each time a project is implemented, more is learned about how to do it more effectively. Useful lessons are learned about what worked and what did not work. That is why Essential Element 5 suggests formative and summative evaluations. It is essential to know whether your project resulted in your intended outcomes and met the expectations of those being served.

Putting first things first when planning a service-learning project makes the entire process run more smoothly, and when that happens, both teachers and students are more likely to be successful. In Chapters 6 and 7, we take a look at specific service-learning activities, understanding that those who developed and implemented these projects did, in fact, do the necessary preparation prior to the students actually doing the service.

5

Team Building
and Reflection

The best way to find yourself is to lose yourself in the service of others.

—Mohandas Gandhi

One of the great benefits of service-learning is its aspect of connecting students to others. When they engage in service-learning, students bond to other students as well as to adults in the school and community. Before asking students to work as team members, it is advisable to help them build relationships based on trust, respect, and understanding of their own diversity. When such relationships are established, students begin the service-learning project better equipped to learn through their reflection on the experience because they are more comfortable sharing thoughts, insights, and feelings in group discussion. Students also feel more likely to ask thoughtful questions in a group setting and give one another honest feedback, criticism, and compliments. Time spent up front on team building pays off in a big way during reflection activities.

TEAM-BUILDING ACTIVITIES FOR K–8 STUDENTS ■

I would like to offer you a few activities that are especially useful in building relationships among students. Through these activities, students have an opportunity to interact in less formal and more intimate ways than they usually do in a school setting. Students get to know one another's likes, dislikes, styles, and talents. The following activities lay a foundation for the development of interpersonal skills and assist students as they work as members of teams.

(Text continues on page 63)

Name of Activity

The Broken Heart

Grade Level

Elementary to middle school, depending on the sophistication of the story chosen

Objective

To help students develop empathy for others

Materials

Large paper hearts, masking tape

Procedure

Give a large paper heart to each student. As you do this, tell the students you will be reading (or telling) them a story and that they should listen for anything that would hurt the feelings of the person in the story. Say that when they hear something hurtful, they should each break off a piece of their paper heart. Then tell or read a story to the class about someone who is having a hard time at home or at school. At the end of the story, have the students put their paper hearts back together again with tape and discuss how the person in the story must have felt.

Discussion

Students have an opportunity to express their feelings about how easy it is for one's feelings to be hurt, and how we ought to be careful of one another's hearts, when you ask them questions like those that follow. Can people's hearts be broken without their showing it on the outside? How do people hide their broken hearts? Once your heart has been broken by words or actions, is it ever the same again? Why or why not? How can we be careful of other people's hearts? Do words hurt more than actions? Can you think of someone who needs us to be more careful with his or her feelings? What will you do to take better care of your heart and others' hearts?

Name of Activity

The Sharing Sack

Grade Level

Elementary to middle school

Objectives

To help students identify their own strengths

To help students recognize strengths in others

Materials

A pair of dice

Index cards with a number written on each card (starting with 2 and ending at 12)

Index cards with a sentence stem written on each card (for example, I'm really good at . . . ; I like myself because . . . ; I did something good when . . .)

Procedure

Have students sit in a circle. Say, "Today we are going to share the good things about ourselves. We are going to talk about our strengths. We sometimes think that when we talk about ourselves in positive ways it means that we are bragging. Today, however, we are not going to worry about that and are just going to describe our individual strengths. We may be good at certain things but not necessarily better than others." Tell the students that they are not to comment on what the other students say. Next give each student a number card, then throw the dice. The student holding that number card goes first. The student reaches into the bag and draws out a card with a sentence stem on it. She or he must complete the sentence with a personal strength. (If a student gets stuck and can't finish the sentence, another student may volunteer to finish the sentence by sharing a strength that she or he sees in that person.) The student then throws the dice for the next person. If there are ten or fewer students in a group, numbers are not repeated as long as everyone gets one turn. If there are more than 10 students in a class, then some numbers would be repeated so that all kids have a turn. In this scenario, more than one student would have the same number, but each student would only take one turn.

Discussion

Ask the students, How did it feel to share good things about yourselves? Did you feel uncomfortable talking about yourselves? Why or why not? What is different about what you were doing here and bragging about yourself? How did it feel if someone completed a sentence for you?

Name of Activity

Cooperative Monster Making

Grade Level

Elementary to middle school

Objectives

To increase ability to work as a member of a team

To form positive relationships and trust among classmates

Materials

Various sheets of colored construction paper, scissors, tape, glue or glue sticks

Four envelopes with four cards inside each (each card has one of these jobs on it—head maker, leg maker, body maker, and arm maker)

Procedure

Tell students that they will be learning about cooperation. Ask them to define the word and give examples. Then, break students up into groups of four, and give each group one envelope with four cards inside, and tell them not to look in the envelopes until you tell them to. When it's time, everyone can take a card from her or his group envelope. Every student then will have one job to do (for example, one person in the group is a head maker, another is the leg maker, etc.). Each group's task is to make a monster. The group decides on what kind of monster they want to make (whether it will be scary or funny, etc.), then each student works on her or his part alone and no one gives suggestions to anyone else unless they are asked to. When everyone is done, each group puts their monster together with tape or glue. The groups then name their monsters and share them with the rest of the class. Hang the monsters around the room.

Discussion

Ask the students questions like these: How did your group cooperate? How was it not being able to give your teammate suggestions? If you could have, would you have made your monster part just like your teammates' parts? Why or why not? What kinds of things did you do in order to cooperate? Why are the monsters so different? How can individual differences make a group better?

Name of Activity Tie Tying Communication Activity
Grade Level Middle school
Objectives To increase students' understanding of communication To help students differentiate between different types of communication To form positive relationships and trust among classmates
Materials Men's ties (enough for students to work in pairs) Cards with tie-tying instructions for those who do not know how to tie a tie A stopwatch
Procedure Tell students that they will be learning about communication and different styles of communicating. Eight students will actively participate—one student will be the timer and the rest of the students will be active observers. The eight students are broken up into pairs. Each pair gets one tie—one student gets the tie and the other one gets the card with instructions, if the student needs it. The first pair of students stands back to back. Tell them that the student with the tie must remain silent. The other student can tell her or him how to tie the tie. No questions or interactions. No looking. The final product is revealed after 3 minutes, finished or not. The rest of the class takes notes on what they observed. The second pair of students stands one facing the other. Tell them that the student with the tie cannot ask questions, but the student giving directions can gesture (but not touch) as she or he gives the directions. After 3 minutes, the final product is revealed, finished or not. Again, the rest of the class observes and takes notes. The third pair of students stands facing each other. This time both students have a tie. The teaching student is going to show the learning student how to tie the tie. No one speaks. Only gestures and observation are allowed. The timer calls time at 3 minutes if the pair has not finished. The product is revealed. The rest of the class observes and takes notes. The fourth pair of students is allowed to face each other and speak to one another. They can ask and answer questions. The timer calls time at 3 minutes if the pair has not finished. The class observes and takes notes.
Discussion Ask the students these questions: What makes communication difficult? How do nonverbal cues enhance or hinder communication? How does communication affect the products we produce? How do misunderstandings occur when people are trying to communicate? What kinds of things get in the way of communication, and what kinds of things make communication easier? Are you more aware of your own style of communication? Do you feel you communicate effectively, or is there an area of communicating that you could work on? Does written communication always help? What did you observe about communication in the various scenarios?

Name of Activity

Broken Sentences

Grade Level

Elementary school

Objectives

To increase students' understanding of nonverbal communication

To increase each student's ability to work as a team member

To form positive relationships and trust among classmates

Materials

Five envelopes for each group of five students. Each envelope has four cards with one word on each as follows:

Envelope 1: spring, loudly, eager, into
Envelope 2: here, burned, ran, the
Envelope 3: is, the, start, reading, the
Envelope 4: fire, bark, I'm, cat, house
Envelope 5: the, me, dogs, to

Procedure

Put students in groups of five, but if students cannot be grouped exactly in groups of five, allow two students to work together with all of the envelopes or give one student two envelopes.

Tell students that they cannot talk to one another during this activity. Give students one envelope each with words in it, and tell them to spread out the words in front of them. Each student must make a sentence that is grammatically correct. There will be five sentences produced by each group.

Each member of the group has her or his own words. A student cannot ask another student for a word, but if a student notices that someone else needs a word, she or he can give one to that person. Group members can see each other's words. All the words must be used, but the sentences do not have to make sense as long as they are grammatically correct.

Some sentences that can be made from the words are: Spring is here. The fire burned me. The dogs bark loudly. I'm eager to start reading. The cat ran into the house. Other sentences can be created—as long as they are grammatically correct.

Discussion

Ask the students these questions: Was it difficult to do this activity without talking? Why? What did your group have to do in order to produce five sentences? Did anyone emerge as the leader? How did it feel to have to give up a word? How did it feel to complete a sentence? What did you learn from this activity?

Name of Activity

What If?

Grade Level

Elementary school

Objectives

To increase students' understanding of the need for rules

To teach students to work cooperatively to establish rules

To form positive relationships and trust among classmates

Materials

"What If" cards with scenarios on them ("What If" cards say things like, What if there were no traffic lights? What if there were no rules for a board game? What if you could go to bed whenever you wanted? What if you only had to work when you wanted? What if you never did your homework? What if you never got a job?)

Newsprint, markers

Procedure

Divide the class into small groups of two or three students, and distribute "What If" cards, markers, and newsprint to the groups. Ask the groups to brainstorm possible outcomes of the situation on their card and write down the outcomes and consequences on newsprint. The groups then share the information on their newsprint with the rest of the class.

   After the groups have shared, the entire class makes a list of class rules. Paraphrase the rules and ask the class to think of the positive and negative consequences of each rule. Have the students vote on the rules they would like to adopt. The rules should then be posted for all to see.

Discussion

Ask the students questions such as, Why are rules important? How would our class run if certain members did not follow the rules? How did it feel to be included in the making of rules and having a say in the consequences? How do adults have a say in the rules that affect them? Do you think that people who vote have a say in the rules? Why or why not?

Name of Activity

The Goodness Gorillas

Grade Level

Elementary school

Objective

To introduce the topic of doing good for others, random acts of kindness

To elicit ideas for projects that students can do

To form positive relationships and trust among classmates

Materials

Chicken Soup for Little Souls: The Goodness Gorillas by Jack Canfield and Mark Victor Hansen

Cards or half sheets of paper, with a story-related question on each one (the questions can be repeated, but there should be enough cards or sheets paper for each student to get one)

Procedure

Tell students that you will read them a story called "The Goodness Gorillas." Give each student a card (or half piece of paper) with a story-related question on it. Tell the students to write the answer to the question on the paper when they hear it in the story. Ask students if they know what "chicken soup for the soul" means? Generally students will say that chicken soup can help you feel better. Tell students that chicken soup stories often help us feel better about life and how people treat each other. Read the story.

Discussion

Ask the students questions such as, How did the Goodness Gorillas get started? What is a random act of kindness? Have students describe three random acts of kindness from the story. Ask, How was Todd different from the other Goodness Gorillas? What sad thing happened to Todd's dog? What did the Goodness Gorillas do for Todd? What do the Goodness Gorillas see in everyone? How did the world become a better place? What is one thing you learned from the story? What types of things could this class, or group, do to make the school a better place? Record ideas and vote on one or two to get started.

Name of Activity

Picture This!

Grade Level

Elementary and middle school

Objectives

To introduce the concept of looking beyond a person's exterior

To form positive relationships and trust among classmates

Materials

One piece of blank paper for each student

Procedure

Ask students to draw a picture of themselves on one side of the paper in 60 seconds. Next tell them to turn the paper over and list as many special or unique things about themselves as they can in 60 seconds. Have students leave their papers on their desks with the picture side up, then stroll around the classroom and look at each other's pictures. Generally this causes lots of laughter.

Discussion

Ask the students these questions: Why did everyone focus so intently on the pictures rather than turning the paper over and looking at each person's unique characteristics? Do we do this in everyday activities? What do we miss by only looking at the exterior of a person? How can we do a better job of finding out about the interior qualities people possess?

Name of Activity

Sign Me Up!

Grade Level

Elementary and middle school

Objectives

To give students a chance to know one another's talents better

To provide information that is useful when assigning jobs to students

To provide choice and voice for students as they consider service projects

Materials

Any number of pieces of large paper hung around the room (each paper has a general or directed statement you've written on it that relates to a student's interests or talents—such as I love working with kids, I really enjoy gardening, I like to organize things, or I enjoy playing a musical instrument)

A marker for each student

Procedure

Tell the students to take their markers and move from one statement to the next until they have had the chance to read them all. When the students read a statement that they feel is true for them, they each sign their name and write a comment, like this: "Sue F.—I like to play the piano and sing" or "Mike D.—I worked with kids this past summer at a day camp." When everyone is finished reading and commenting on the statements, you ask a student who has signed a particular statement to read what has been written by those who have signed that sheet.

Discussion

Ask the students questions such as, What can we say about our group as a whole? What different talents are represented? What different interests do you see? Did we forget to ask about any other interests? What types of projects could we consider with the talents and interests represented in this group? Was there a chart that had no signers? What does that indicate? What was the most interesting comment made?

REFLECTION ACTIVITIES ■

Reflection and process activities are the keys to successful service-learning. Critical reflection provides the transformational link between serving and learning. Reflection solidifies the experience in the students' minds and deepens learning. Time constraints being what they are, it is sometimes tempting to wing it. This is not a good idea because the effectiveness of critical reflection depends on someone taking responsibility for making it happen (Eyler, Giles, & Schmiede, 1996).

Make sure you know how you will incorporate reflection into your activity. Will you process it each time you have a service experience? Will you have students journal after each experience? Will you have discussions? Will students make presentations or create visuals? What choices will you offer for students? If you make reflection a priority, it will get done. If you do not, it may get pushed aside by the activity itself, and students will miss out on wonderful learning opportunities.

Reflection can take many forms. It can occur through discussion, written reports, journaling, drawing, music, role-playing, and more. Reflection can be structured by giving specific questions that students must respond to, or it can be made more open-ended by allowing students to draw their own conclusions. The students' grade level will influence the type of reflection chosen. Elementary students often need more structured guidance for their reflection than older students do.

Teachers need to choose their reflection activity based on their learning objective and the time available to them. By engaging in quality reflection, students gain enormous opportunities for deepening their understanding and connecting their learning to their lives. Asking students the following questions can lead them into interesting before and after service-learning reflections.

Before the Service-Learning Activity

- What do you think you will find when we go to our site today?
- What will the people be like, and what kinds of things do you think they will want to do?
- What special needs do you think the people there might have?

After the Service-Learning Activity

- What interesting thing happened at your site today?
- Why do you suppose that person acted that way?
- Tell us about your experience and what happened.
- How did you feel after your experience?
- What things would you do differently the next time?
- What have you learned about yourself from this experience?
- What do you think the people you served thought about your help?
- How will you use this experience in your own life?

- What aspects of theory did you observe in action today?
- What did you notice about what we learned in class when you got to the site?
- What things that we learned about in class did you observe at the service site?
- What do you think will happen next time when you do some things differently?

Reflection does not have to be time-consuming or complicated. It does have to be effective and meaningful. The key is to choose reflection activities that help students understand not only subject content but also their strengths and their personal contributions.

Table 5.1 offers some structure for deciding the type of reflection activity that would be appropriate for your needs and time constraints.

Table 5.1   Reflective Teaching Strategies

Type	Primary Result	Description
Reading and creative projects	Foster group bonding and leadership; facilitate directed learning	Essays, music, videos, artwork
Journal writing	Fosters personal growth	Students maintain a regular journal that the faculty member reads and responds to
Directed writing	Fosters directed growth	Students produce essays that address specific questions or issues specified by the instructor
Feelings-oriented oral reflection	Fosters group bonding and trust	Class members participate in a group discussion regarding their service experiences
Student as expert oral reflection	Fosters citizenship, leadership, and cognitive learning	Students lead a session providing a critique of a reading assignment or a solution to a problem
Cognitive teaching oral reflection	Fosters leadership, directed learning, cognitive learning, personal growth, and critical thinking	Teacher leads a teaching session that fosters critical thinking and problem solving

Source: Silcox (1995).

THE CYCLE OF REFLECTION ■

David Kolb (1984), who is noted for his work with experiential education, offers a model for reflection that can be extremely useful when processing service-learning experiences. It is a cyclical model that begins with *having the actual experience*. Then discussion centers on processing that experience by *recounting facts* related to the experience. Once that is done, the discussion moves to *creating a hypothesis regarding the experience* drawing from what was learned. The reflection ends with the person's *testing this hypothesis the next time* he or she has a similar experience, and the process repeats itself, each time with deepened understanding and learning (see Figure 5.1). This model is useful to help students reflect on their experiences, what they have learned, and what they will do differently next time.

Figure 5.1   Kolb's Experiential Learning Cycle

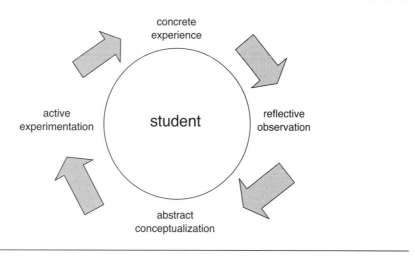

Source: Eyler, Giles, and Schmiede (1996).

REFLECTION ACTIVITIES FOR ■ YOUNGER STUDENTS

The following reflection activities can be very useful with elementary and middle school students who often do better with structured than with unstructured activities to guide their reflection.

Name of Activity

The Amnesia Game

Grade Level

Elementary and middle school

Objectives

To offer students the opportunity to receive positive feedback from peers

To enhance students' ability to observe one another's behavior and contributions to the project

To help students see that each person on a project has something to offer

Materials

None

Procedure

Have the members of the class or service-learning group sit in a large circle. Choose one student to pretend to have lost all memory of the service-learning experience and her or his role in it. The rest of the group must refresh this student's memory. Group members must specifically state things that the person did during the service-learning experience, such as, "I saw you playing bingo with the lady in the wheelchair," "I saw you being very gentle with a third grader," or "You are always on time and ready to go."

Group members must try to identify the behaviors and attitudes that contributed to the success of the project. You should be sure there is enough trust in the group to handle constructive criticism before you allow group members to make critical comments. If there is not enough trust, then tell the group that comments should stay positive and that those who cannot think of something positive to say should say "Pass." The amnesia victim can ask questions, if she or he would like more insight or does not understand what someone has said.

Discussion

Ask the students these questions: Were you surprised that people knew so much about the behavior and attitude of this one student? What does this tell you about people? Why is it important to be aware of the impact of your behavior? What were some of the comments that you found most helpful? What things do most people remember about another? How would you like to be remembered? Will you change any behavior as a result of this information? Will you do anything even more often?

Name of Activity

The New Me

Grade Level

Elementary and middle school

Objectives

To assist students in identifying what they have learned about themselves and their subject content as a result of the service-learning experience

To assist students in planning for future actions

To foster discussion among students as they share their pictures

To identify commonalities among students in order to enhance social bonding

Materials

Newsprint or another type of paper

Procedure

Have each student draw a gingerbread-like figure to represent herself or himself. When all the students have finished drawing, give them the following directions: Near the head, write the things you learned while doing the service-learning activity. Near the hands, write the things you actually did during the activity. Near the heart, write how you feel about what you did and the people you interacted with or helped. Near the legs and feet, write what you will do from now on to continue to learn and help others.

Discussion

Hang the pictures around the room or share them individually. Students can pair and share in small groups as well. When people have finished sharing, ask them what the common ideas are in the statements on the pictures. Ask, Do many of us feel similar feelings about the experience? What is most common? What is the most unique statement made? How can we make sure that we actually do the things we said we would? How can we help one another stay on track?

Name of Activity

The Learning Tree

Grade Level

Any grade

Objectives

To provide a visual representation of students' academic and personal learning as a result of the service-learning experience

To help students identify and express what they have learned

Materials

A large tree without leaves, cut out and placed on a bulletin board or wall

A quantity of two different colors of Post-it notes

Procedure

After a service activity is completed, ask students to write on pink Post-it notes something that they learned about themselves and on yellow Post-it notes something that they learned about the subject matter. Tell students that they may write as many Post-it notes as they wish. Give each student a chance to read to the group all of the notes she or he has written. Then stick all the Post-it notes onto a large tree on the bulletin board or on a wall so everyone can admire the colorful learning that has taken place.

Discussion

Ask the students questions such as, What do you notice about the colors? Is one more plentiful than another? What is your opinion of learning about yourself and learning about a subject at the same time? What did you learn about how you like to learn?

Elementary students can also use short questionnaires such as the one below to reflect on their learning experience. The one below is just an example, so teachers will need to tailor the questions to relate to their own students' experience and subject content.

Elementary School Students' Reflection Sheet

Name _____ Date _____

1. What job did you do today at the service site?

2. Name some people you worked with.

3. What did you learn today about _____ from your service-learning project?

4. What did you learn today about yourself?

5. Now that you know that, what will you do differently next time?

6. Finish this sentence: This program would be better if . . .

REFLECTION FOR OLDER STUDENTS ■

As students mature, their reflection becomes more sophisticated. The following list of questions can be used in any number of ways to direct discussion, provoke thinking, and guide students as they demonstrate their learning. Students could write responses to the questions, discuss them in a group, draw or musically represent their answers, take photographs (with permission), create collages, or show their reflections in some other way.

Questions for Reflection

1. What job did you have today at the service site?

2. What communication skills did you use?

3. What new things did you learn today about your partner?

4. What new things did you learn about yourself?

5. Would you do anything differently next time?

6. How did what we learned in class help you today at the service site?

7. Did you learn anything today during service that will help you with class work?

8. Has this experience changed your opinions in any way?

9. Do you have any interest in learning more about a career in this area?

10. When you think about this experience, what is the most important thing you have learned?

11. What has surprised you about this experience?

12. How will you apply your new insights to your life?

13. How did service to others make you feel?

14. Were there instances when you were afraid or nervous?

15. How did you deal with your nervousness? What helped you to overcome it?

16. If you worked as a member of a team, how did your team function?

17. What did you learn about your community from participating in this project?

18. Is there something you can do now that you could not do before?

19. What risks did you take during this project?

20. What did you learn about yourself from taking a risk today?

21. What advice do you have for anyone considering service-learning?

Collecting feedback from students is a way to assess the impact of the service-learning experience, as well as a form of reflection. A questionnaire like the one below can be done individually by students and then handed in or discussed in a small group. Again, the following questionnaire is just an example, so teachers will need to customize their questions to fit the objectives of their service-learning projects.

Middle School Students' Service-Learning Evaluation

Directions: Please circle the number that best describes your opinion.

1. Being part of service-learning increased my self-confidence (that is, helped me feel like I can do things).

1	2	3	4
NO!	No	Yes	YES!

2. Being part of service-learning helped me become more responsible (by showing up to meetings, being serious about the funding decisions, etc.).

1	2	3	4
NO!	No	Yes	YES!

3. I felt like I belonged to the service-learning group.

1	2	3	4
NO!	No	Yes	YES!

4. Being part of service-learning helped me learn things that I will need for a job or school (like being on time, working with others, reading assignments, and talking about ideas).

1	2	3	4
NO!	No	Yes	YES!

5. Being part of service-learning gave me a chance to make things better in the community.

1	2	3	4
NO!	No	Yes	YES!

6. Being part of service-learning gave me a chance to spend time with some caring adults.

1	2	3	4
NO!	No	Yes	YES!

7. Learning schoolwork through service-learning is helpful to me.

1	2	3	4
NO!	No	Yes	YES!

8. I have found school to be more enjoyable since I have been doing service-learning.

1	2	3	4
NO!	No	Yes	YES!

9. My grades have improved since I have been doing service-learning.

1	2	3	4
NO!	No	Yes	YES!

10. Being a part of service-learning helped me learn new things about myself like . . .

■ FINAL WORDS

As the Essential Elements have indicated, preparation for the service-learning experience is essential. Students have to be prepared for the service itself, and they also have to be prepared through team-building activities that help them to form strong relationships with each other. In addition to team building, reflection is of utmost importance. Students need different reflective activities at different grade levels, moving from very concrete to more abstract. When teachers pay attention to both ends of the service-learning experience, preparation and reflection, students derive the most benefit.

6

Service-Learning Projects That Put Learning First

I learned that I can do things I never thought I could.

—Fifth grade student

The five projects that follow are being offered to readers as possibilities. Counselors or teacher-advisers, rather than teachers in a classroom setting, implemented many of the projects below. As each project is presented, I will explain how the ideas presented can be adapted by teachers for classroom use.

Many of the projects involved helping students who needed to be more connected to school and/or who needed to develop socially. However, the projects also engaged students who already possessed these attributes and enhanced their personal skills and learning. It is my hope that one or more of the projects will plant a seed or spark an idea in you that will lead to action.

Rather than offer a cookbook approach with an exact recipe for service-learning, I offer examples of actual service activities that are quite varied. As you read, think about the content in your curricula and imagine how you could adapt elements of these examples to your own set of circumstances.

High-quality service-learning is connected to learning standards and curriculum, and you will see how each of the examples below enhances students' achievement of learning objectives. Both students' personal development and their learning were enhanced through these projects. If teachers had initiated the projects rather than counselors, subject content would have determined the type of projects done. In the models that follow, the goals—students' personal development and connection to school—determined the desired outcomes, and subject content was a secondary focus. Teachers can turn that around and let increased learning and subject content determine the desired outcomes, while personal and social development develop secondarily.

As you read about these projects, consider how you can make your content come alive with the addition of service-learning projects. I hope that these examples will help your creative juices start flowing. Each of the following examples is described and then outlined in a chart format. I have not included celebrations on the charts, but each of these projects incorporated celebration in some way. The key to a celebration of service-learning is giving students an opportunity to showcase in a variety of ways what they have learned and accomplished through their service. Remember that the learning and the accomplishment of a goal is what we are celebrating. Be sure to invite parents and community partners!

■ SCHOOL STORE PROGRAM

This program was originally designed for students who were identified by a school counselor as needing to increase their social skills and connection to school. The counselor decided that reopening their closed school store would be a great project. The students have now operated the school store successfully for 3 years, and the program is still going strong.

This store is located on the main floor of a small elementary school. It is open two mornings per week, before the students take their seats in their classrooms. Students involved with the project make the decisions regarding what to sell from catalogues provided by their counselor. Some of those items include pencils, paper, erasers, notebooks, crayons, and other school supplies. They also sell candy and key chains and other novelty items. The students count out the money at the end of each day, record what was sold, and compute profits. The counselor then takes the money box to the office for safekeeping.

This particular small group has had good attendance, especially on "store" days. The students have an incentive to keep their homework and class work up-to-date because their participation in the program depends on it. Overall, their classroom teacher reports that the students in the program have developed more confidence in themselves, and that is what the counselor was hoping for.

Adaptation

Even though this activity originated with a counselor working with a small group of identified students, it could easily be adapted for an entire class project. An entire unit of study could use the store as its focal point. Math computation skills and the social interaction skills of listening and speaking that are part of English and language arts could be honed. The career skills associated with a retail business, teamwork, and exploring career options could be integrated into the project. Teachers could form committees and assign students tasks to do, such as decorating the store, arranging merchandise, advertising, and so on. Students could rotate turns serving as clerks, salespeople, inventory specialists, accountants, and clean-up crews. The entire class could assume responsibility for decorating the store thematically and deciding on items to carry for sale.

Teamwork

It is always a challenge to get students to know, respect, and cooperate with one another. Students have a natural tendency to form groups that include some and exclude others. To overcome this tendency, you will need to spend some pre-project time doing team-building exercises so that the group can become more cohesive. Respect for one another, honesty, and responsibility should be emphasized. The lesson plan that follows is an example of a simple activity that can begin the process of kids getting to know each other better. (See Chapter 5 for more team-building activities.)

Name of Activity Just Like Me
Grade Level All grade levels
Objective To help students get to know one another and develop interpersonal comfort
Materials Student-created lists of five to ten statements to be read to the rest of the class or group
Procedure In this activity, the students take turns leading the group by reading all of their statements. The leaders' statements should be true for them, and if any of the statements are also true for any of the rest of the group, those people are invited to stand and say, "Just like me." For example, the leader might say, "I love to sleep late on Saturday mornings." If that statement is true for others in the group, they stand and say together, "Just like me." They then sit and wait for the next statement. The leader then might say, "I really love to read books." The group then reacts to that statement. As you might imagine, the statements can be serious or funny. They may involve leaders taking a risk in revealing something about themselves. They can help students to know one another better. Students take turns being the leader—and developing statements that the rest of the group will react to—until all the students have had an opportunity to participate. (If the level of trust in the class is

low, you might consider collecting all of the statements and reading them aloud without identifying who said them. You could then identify the author after students stood up. This would eliminate the problem of students not standing for fear of being seen as like someone they consider "not cool." By experiencing the activity this way, students might be surprised to see that they actually have something in common with a person they do not like or do not know very well.)

Discussion

Ask the students questions such as, How does it feel to know there are others who feel just like you? Did anything surprise you today? Did you learn anything new about someone in the room?

Necessary Skills

Running a store sounds easier to students than it really is. Many students do not understand the basics of customer relations. It is important to take time to teach the skills of customer interaction, such as being polite and being helpful, since kids do not always have these skills modeled for them at home. Handling money is another critical skill. Some students learn to handle money and make change more quickly than others, and since it is necessary to ensure that this is a successful experience for all, some students may require one-on-one tutorials.

The Project Logistics

The core aspects of this project are identified in the chart that follows.

Name of Activity

School Store Program

Grade Level

All secondary grades, but especially fifth and sixth grades

Objectives

To increase students' social skills

To foster positive relationships among peers

To strengthen students' connection to school

To increase students' self-efficacy, confidence, and responsibility

To reinforce students' mathematical skills, decision making, and teamwork

To reinforce students' English and language arts skills of speaking and listening in social interactions

To reinforce students' career development skills of teamwork and exploring career options

Learning Standards Supported by This Activity

English and language arts—reading; writing, listening, and speaking as social interactions

Career development and occupational standards—applying academic learning in the workplace and other settings; working as a member of a team; exploring career options

Mathematics—understanding and applying mathematical concepts and principles; making change, computing costs, budget development

Preparation Necessary for Program Implementation

If this activity is done as a leadership program for identified students:

- Consult with teachers or principals to determine which students could benefit from the experience.
- Create and send out permission slips to the students' parents.

If this activity is done for *either* identified students or a classroom service project:

- Secure start-up funds for purchasing goods to be sold, possibly from the PTA.
- Prepare team-building activities for the students.
- Secure catalogues for ordering store inventory.
- Prepare the store for operation: clean the area, display materials, set up an accounting system, and find a money box or cash register.
- Schedule times for the school store to be open.
- Enlist the assistance of at least one other adult who can help supervise store operations.

Preliminary Student Preparation

- Students need to learn to work together. Initial icebreaker and team-building activities must occur to ensure that students know, respect, and understand one another.
- Using catalogues, students need to work together to decide what materials to buy and sell.
- Students need to learn how to develop a plan for job assignments and for how to solve problems that arise.
- Students need to know how to log in merchandise, how to make change, how to speak to customers, how to keep a neat store, how to tally sales for the day, how to take inventory, and how to determine if profits were made.

Activity Summary

- The intention of the project is explained to students, including the need for them to work as members of small teams.
- Either in small groups or as a class, students initially participate in team-building exercises designed to help them get to know and trust one another and learn to cooperate. They might also name the store and decorate it according to a theme.

An adult is present for guidance, but students assume responsibility for all of the tasks, as follows:

- Students spend time looking over catalogues of materials to buy and making decisions about which ones are best.
- Students plan, problem-solve, and operate the store, taking turns in small groups of four students at a time per day.
- Students tally profits at the end of each day and the money is kept safe with the supervising adult.
- Students take inventory and place orders when supplies get low.

Assessment

- Teachers and administrators provide feedback on student performance.
- Customers fill out a satisfaction survey.
- Teachers respond to and grade student class assignments related to the project.
- Students complete a questionnaire to assess their own perceptions of growth.

Reflection

- During store hours, informal discussions occur between the supervising adult and the students regarding how students perceive the job and their performance.
- Students write about their experiences as part of a graded assignment. Reflection questions are provided for the students.

■ FREEDOM GARDEN PROJECT

This project began after 9/11. In discussions that followed the tragic events of that day, elementary students who were part of a peer leadership program in the school wondered what they could do in response to show that they cared about those who lost their lives. The students who made up this peer leadership group were chosen based on a variety of criteria. Some students were chosen because they needed to form positive social skills, and others were chosen to be positive role models. Some needed to develop a connection to school, others needed to connect with a caring adult. There were also students who showed leadership potential but needed that potential directed in more positive ways.

The teacher-adviser suggested that they plant a memorial garden as a tribute to those who died on 9/11, and the students jumped at the idea. The idea became a long-term project that started in November and ended in June. This particular group of peer leaders had already been visiting a local senior citizen center to serve the seniors lunch and play games with them. The teacher-adviser was able to use this established relationship to enhance the new garden project. She had students and seniors plant seeds together, and while they did that, students asked questions about gardening and learned the best way to care for their garden from the seniors. The students could have done library research on flowers or interviewed nursery or greenhouse gardeners to obtain this information, but time constraints prohibited this. Instead, their counselor chose to give the students the opportunity to learn about caring for the garden from the seniors, thus also reinforcing existing relationships between the students and the seniors.

The students started their project by working in teams to design how the garden would look. They discussed it and wrote about their ideas. Then they voted on the best design and all agreed to work on it. They chose a site for the garden and got permission from the principal to move forward. All the students wrote letters to local businesses soliciting donations for the garden, and the teacher-adviser chose the ones to send. Some students made dioramas with colored clay to illustrate the placement of the various flowers. Later in the project, students wrote letters to parents and other important people inviting them to the dedication ceremony. This peer leadership group was only able to meet weekly throughout the school year, so this project took longer to complete than it would have if the group could have met more frequently.

Adaptation

Even though this project was done by a group of about 40 peer leaders, it could easily be adapted as a classroom project. It has elements of science, civics, math, and English and language arts built right in. Students learned about the life of a plant, how plants need sun and water to grow, which plants make the most colorful gardens, and which plants thrive in the sun. They learn that a group of committed people can make a beautiful contribution to their community with their effort. Students learn about measurement, area, and perimeter. They determine what materials they will need for the garden and how much the garden will cost. They find out how many inches apart to place plants so they will grow well. They also learn to write letters to businesses and to write letters of invitation.

Classroom teachers who wish to replicate this project could separate their classes into smaller groups, or committees, and break up the responsibilities. Some steps could be done as an entire class, and some steps could be done in smaller groups. For example, part of the class could do silent reading while the other part is planting or caring for their seedlings. The students' math assignments could revolve around the project.

Students could interview professional gardeners to learn about their businesses and ask questions about which plants make good borders and so on.

They could also find out the type of education or experience one needs to do this kind of work. This research could be useful in the planning of their own garden, and it may open possibilities for their future career options.

Caveat

It is advisable to have a few extra adults present during the actual in-ground planting to help guide students. And, since gardening is a big commitment, maintaining the garden could remain an ongoing project for classes that follow.

The Project Logistics

The core aspects of this project are identified in the chart that follows.

Name of Activity

Freedom Garden Project

Grade Level

Grades 4–8

Objectives

To plant a memorial garden on school grounds that commemorates and beautifies

To teach students to work as members of a cooperative group

To form social relationships among students

To enhance students' connectedness to school

To increase students' self-esteem and self-efficacy

To increase students' bonding to community

To connect students to the larger society

To reinforce science standards related to the life cycle of plants, photosynthesis, irrigation, etc.

To reinforce math standards related to practical math skills: measurement, area, perimeter, budgeting, estimation, computation

To use English/language arts skills to write letters and invitations

To reinforce civic responsibility and pride in students

Learning Standards Supported by This Activity

English and language arts—reading and writing; listening and speaking in social interactions

Career development and occupational standards—applying academic learning in the workplace and other settings (teamwork, cooperation, knowledge of systems)

Mathematics—understanding and applying mathematical concepts and principles: measurement, area, perimeter, budgeting, and cost computation

Social studies—learning about citizenship and civic responsibility

Science—learning about the life cycle of a plant, photosynthesis, irrigation

Preparation Necessary for Program Implementation

- Meet with the principal to get permission and discuss plans for the garden.
- Determine a location for the garden on school grounds.
- Plan times for students to meet with the seniors at the community center (or other identified experts) to discuss planting seeds and gardening basics.
- Prepare a list of local businesses (with their addresses) from which to solicit donations for the garden.
- Determine the approximate cost of the garden based on its size.

Preliminary Student Preparation

- Students need to discuss the garden and its purpose.
- Students need to create a timeline of when activities are to take place.

Activity Summary

- Students meet for 1 hour per week to work on this project.
- Students submit designs for the garden. The group votes for one design.
- Students choose a garden site. They decide how large the garden should be and take measurements of the site. Once the size of the garden has been determined, students help compute the cost of garden.
- Students create a clay diorama of the garden and share it with the rest of the school.
- Students brainstorm a list of supplies needed for the gardening project.
- Students write letters to local businesses to solicit items needed for the garden.
- Students brainstorm fundraising ideas, then implement the fundraiser with permission from their parents.
- Students plan a Freedom Garden Dedication for June. They brainstorm a guest list, music, food, decorations, and an agenda. Students write letters requesting supplies and food.
- Students gather gardening materials for the project with money from donations and the fundraiser. They plant seeds for flowers with seniors at the center, after researching which flowers will thrive in the amount and hours of sunlight available in the garden. They care for the seedlings.
- Students prepare the land for the garden.
- If students choose to, they can build flower boxes—for example, two star-shaped boxes and one flag-shaped box. (Handy parents or even local carpentry classes may be able to help out here.)
- Students plant flowers in the boxes and place finishing touches such as mulch.
- Students create a memorial plaque for the victims of 9/11 and those who fought for freedom.
- In June, there is a celebration of the completion of the Freedom Garden.
- Continual care of the garden is needed, so this project will go on and next year's peer leaders will have work to do.

Assessment

- Teachers complete a survey with their observations of students since their involvement with service-learning.
- Students complete a questionnaire asking about their perception of how well they worked as group members, and whether they perceive their school experience to have improved as a result of their service-learning.
- The teacher keeps notes of improvement in individual students' behavior using the progress chart in Figure 6.1 on page 84.

Reflection

- Students complete reflection sheets to assess how they felt being a part of this project and how it has changed them.
- Students complete "I learned" statements and participate in group discussions.

Assessment

The following is an example of an assessment tool that can be used to assess the impact of this program on students. This is a teacher-made tool that includes statements that are related to the objectives of the project.

Student's Self-Assessment

Name _____   Date _____

As a result of participating in the Freedom Garden project, I have learned

1. That it is important to remember in some visible way those in our society who have suffered or who have made sacrifices for our benefit.

       Yes   No   Maybe

2. To know and understand the students in my classroom better.

       Yes   No   Maybe

3. To work as a member of a group and how to accomplish things as a group.

       Yes   No   Maybe

4. To understand math better (like area, perimeter, and estimating).

       Yes   No   Maybe

5. To understand how plants grow and how to care for them.

   Yes   No   Maybe

6. To understand that growing plants and making gardens is a job I might like.

   Yes   No   Maybe

7. Finish this statement: What I liked (or didn't like) about this program was

8. Finish this statement: If I could change one thing it would be

It is important to keep track of students' individual progress. The form in Figure 6.1 can be kept with the regular attendance sheet and used initially to identify specific behaviors that need improvement and later, when the project is complete, to assess whether improvement occurred. The last segment is for students who do not present with problem behavior. Teachers record there whether students have enhanced their positive traits through this project.

"I CARE" KITS FOR THE HOMELESS ■

This project was started by a teacher who works with identified youngsters in a peer leadership program within an inner-city school. Students collect toiletry items for the needy and homeless and deliver them to the shelter for distribution. Students are chosen to participate in this activity for a variety of reasons, including problems with social skills, attachment to school, and confidence. Students who excel in these areas are included in the group as positive role models. This project is appropriate for students in many different grade levels, including high school.

Because this particular project includes a visit by students to the homeless shelter so that they can deliver goods and serve a breakfast meal, they get a chance to meet homeless people face-to-face. Students who have participated in this activity reported that they were surprised to learn that some homeless people are clean and dress nicely. They learned that homeless people are just

Figure 6.1 Service-Learning Progress Chart

Group Identification _____

Begin Date _____   End Date _____

Name of student	Has this student shown difficulty working with others?	Has this student's ability to work as a member of a group improved?	Has this student shown a need to form positive relationships?	Has this student's ability to form positive relationships improved?	Has this student had problems with school performance?	Has this student's school performance improved?	Has student enhanced existing positive skills and connections?

like them, that they have feelings and hope—and even offer advice to others. The students reported feeling good that they had helped others. The parents of the students who participated in this project were very supportive. One parent said it was the best educational activity her child has experienced at school.

At the beginning of this project, a representative from a shelter for the homeless comes to school to speak to the students about the issue of homelessness. Later in the project, as part of their responsibilities, students go into classrooms and make presentations. After learning about the extent of the problem, students include facts in their presentations about the number of people in their community who need assistance. They ask students in other classes to bring items to school to donate to the homeless. The students involved in the project gain valuable public speaking experience through this activity.

Adaptation

Classroom teachers could integrate this project into course content related to economics, drug abuse, poverty, the Great Depression, and health, to name a few. Students could learn how the loss of a job could result in homelessness for a person or an entire family. They could also learn how important it is to make good decisions regarding use of substances—for both health and economic reasons. Students could do research on resilient people who have fallen into dire straights and emerged whole again. This project could be related to literature in many ways, since some of our greatest stories center on the Great Depression. How quickly our country moved from the era of *The Great Gatsby* to the era of *The Grapes of Wrath!* Students might consider whether that could ever happen again.

Classroom teachers could develop assignments related to this project that would give students an awareness of the amount of money it takes to live in this society. Computing the value of the donated items, finding out how much rent costs, and finding out how much people must set aside each month for heat, lights, food, and clothing are simple assignments that would hone math skills. This would also increase students' awareness of how a person who lacks education or skills is at a disadvantage economically. Students would begin to understand the practical value of education, and how any unexpected event, such as a factory closing, could be catastrophic for those who are affected by it economically. They could also learn that our government has safeguards—such as unemployment benefits, food stamps, and welfare—that are in place to help people who are faced with a crisis. Students would gain an understanding of how our government works in humanitarian ways and how people ought to use those benefits responsibly.

This could be a direct service-learning project in which students visit the local shelter to deliver their kits and meet the people who receive them. Or, if transportation is a problem, it could be an indirect service-learning project in which students collect goods brought to the school site but do not deliver the donations personally.

Name of Activity

"I Care" Kits for the Homeless

Grade Level

Elementary and middle school

Objectives

To develop students' awareness of the homeless problem

To develop students' empathy for the homeless and less fortunate

To teach students the different causes of homelessness

To teach students to work cooperatively to complete a project

To increase students' community connection and awareness of civic duty

To increase students' self-efficacy

To support learning associated with history and economics

Learning Standards Supported by This Activity

Social studies—learning about civics and citizenship, the Great Depression and economics, and social benefit systems

Health—making wise personal, health, and safety choices

English and language arts—reading; writing, listening, and speaking as social interactions; literature related to this topic

Math—understanding the amount of money it takes to feed, clothe, and shelter an individual or family, estimating and computation

Preparation Necessary for Program Implementation

- Contact local shelters. Ask if "I Care" Kits could be used by their clients and ask for other ways students might help.

- Meet with the principal and enlist support from classroom teachers.

- Create a schedule for classroom presentations on the project.

- Collect boxes to hold donations.

- Get donations of plastic grocery bags from local supermarkets.

- Arrange transportation to and from the shelter.

- Create feedback forms for getting information from students, parents, and teachers.

- Create a schedule for morning announcements.

- Create a volunteer chart for various student responsibilities.

- Buy samples of travel-size personal care products as examples.

Preliminary Student Preparation

- Students need to learn about the homeless in the community, so ask a representative from a local shelter to come to school and tell students about them.
- Students need to understand that they can help the homeless, so after the presentation, ask them what they learned and for ideas of ways they could help and present the idea of "I Care" Kits.
- Students need to know about hygiene and the reasons why everyone needs to keep their teeth, hair, body, and skin clean.
- If you are integrating this activity into subject content, students need to understand the connection between the community activity and what they are learning (for example, the origins of soup kitchens in this country during the Great Depression, health and hygiene, etc.).

Activity Summary

- Students brainstorm the list of necessary items for collection.
- Students prepare and make presentations to classes to enlist their help with collection.
- Students make posters informing others about the homeless and requesting donations for them. They hang the posters in hallways and classrooms.
- Students decorate collection boxes.
- Students collect donations for 2 weeks (or more).
- Students remind other students and teachers to make donations by making morning announcements.
- When the collection is done, students sort items and fill bags with goods.
- Students deliver the bags to the shelter and participate in serving a meal to the homeless.
- If possible, pictures are taken during the serving of the meal.

Assessment

This project as it is currently implemented does not include assessment. However, if you are a teacher integrating course content into the project, your assessment would be connected to particular assignments. Students work on math, reading, social studies, and health through this project and have the chance to apply their learning to a real-life situation. Tests and written assignments could serve as the assessment of student achievement of learning objectives. Reflection activities would further enhance the students' critical thinking and personal development.

Reflection

- After the trip to the shelter, students discuss the experience. Feelings, perceptions of the homeless, and what was learned are discussed.
- When the film is developed, posters are made with students writing a short description of each picture. (This is optional.)
- Students go back to the classrooms with their posters to describe the experience and what they learned. They also make a bulletin board with pictures of the day.

■ AFRICAN-AMERICAN VISUAL MUSEUM

A counselor working with a large group of youngsters in an inner-city elementary school created this project. Students who participated were in the fourth and fifth grades. Their task was to research and study African-American culture, create displays similar to those in a museum, and then conduct tours of their displays for other classes within the school. They were to explain their displays and teach other students about African culture and the contributions made by African Americans to our culture. Any culture could have been chosen, but this school is predominately African American, and therefore that culture was most interesting to the students. Also, the counselor was interested in instilling in the students pride in their own culture.

The counselor who created this project chose to include both positive and painful aspects of African Americans' history and experience, from the kings and queens of Africa to enslavement to the present. By starting the students' historical journey with royalty, the counselor's intention was to instill pride in their culture in her young students, who were used to hearing about Africans' enslavement rather than their glorious past. Eventually the students did learn about their ancestors' being enslaved, and their contributions to this country both during and after this dark time. The counselor emphasized that during their enslavement, the Africans demonstrated important life skills such as perseverance, courage, problem solving, empathy, and caring.

The teacher-adviser offered students the choice of which periods of African-American history they wanted to research and make displays about. Topics included kings and queens, the Middle Passage, and African-American inventors. In that way, students were given a choice for their study and a voice in the type of display that they would create. They worked in small groups, so they learned how to work as a team.

These are some of the comments made by the fifth grade participants in the project:

> "I learned that the slaves jumped off the slave ship so they didn't have to come to America."

> "There were kids on the ship and they were all chained together."

> "Some of the people on the ship fought back. They were really brave."

> "I learned we were kings and queens."

> "I didn't know a black man invented the helicopter."

The excitement created by this project was well worth the effort that it took. A fifth grade teacher made this comment about one of the students who participated in the project: "The project has been great for S. She has really gained a lot of confidence. She was so excited to show the classes around."

Adaptation

This project could be adapted in many different ways, and it could easily be adapted for higher grades. It could be a project for an entire classroom of students, rather than a select group, and it could focus on many different cultures or on subject topics such as science. The museum could be a schoolwide project with each class focusing on a certain topic or culture. The students' work would be displayed, and they would take turns playing docent. This project could be used in special subjects (such as art, music, and library) as a focal point around which to revolve content in the lessons, thus reinforcing learning as well as showcasing students' work in the museum.

Individual classroom teachers could use the African-American culture (or any worthy topic) as a theme for study that all of their subjects could focus on. Math, reading, science, and social studies assignments could be related to this topic, and students could create displays of their knowledge for their museums. In upper grades where students have more than one teacher, the teachers for individual subjects could coordinate their curricula so that, for example, an English teacher would assign reading that would reinforce what the social studies teacher was teaching. All the teachers on a team ought to be able to coordinate their assignments and content so that students can see the thematic connection within all subjects. Applying skills is much more meaningful when students are working on a project that interests them and that they enjoy. The critical aspects of the project are in the chart below.

Name of Activity

African American Visual Museum (Students research African-American history and create displays to illustrate it, then give tours of their museum to the other classes in the school.)

Grade Level

Middle school

Objectives

To teach students to speak, read and write as social interactions

To teach students important facts about history and important people in history

To form positive social relationships among students

To increase students' knowledge of and pride in their heritage

To increase students' self-efficacy

To help students bond to their school community

To reinforce students' learning in subject areas such as social studies, reading, math, and science

Learning Standards Supported by This Activity

English and language arts—reading; writing, listening, and speaking as social interactions and to increase understanding

Career development and occupational studies—learning teamwork and cooperation

Social studies—learning about African-American history

Math—learning computation skills

Preparation Necessary for Program Implementation

- Meet with the principal to ask permission for the museum.
- Discuss plans with all the affected teachers and ask for their support.
- Raise funds if money will be needed to buy materials.
- Do preliminary research into possible topic areas that students might choose from.

Preliminary Student Preparation

- Students need to discuss the idea of the museum.
- Students need to discuss the timeline of the events they will be showcasing: pre-enslavement to present day contributors.
- Students should choose a time period or project they want to work on.
- Students need to learn about museum displays and what they include. (Students would benefit from a visit to a museum and an exhibit they could use as a model for their display, but this is not essential.)

Activity Summary

The project begins in January and ends in June, and it proceeds as follows:

- Fundraising takes place if money is needed.
- The teacher purchases the materials required by students as they work on their project.
- Students break into groups of three or four and choose a topic to research and create a museum display for. (For example, these are some of the topics for this project: kings and queens of Africa, the Middle Passage, community living, African-American inventors, Civil Rights Movement, and past and present-day contributors.)
- Students research their areas and create displays and handouts for visitors.
- Students and teachers choose a date for the museum tours. Students act as tour guides explaining the significance of the displays and answering any questions the classes have.

Assessment

This project did not include assessment of academic learning because it was an enrichment activity primarily designed to connect students to school. However, if it were adapted by a classroom teacher, assessment of learning would take place through graded tests on the content that the students were working on through their creation of the museum. Assessment of the value of the project itself could be done by surveying teachers and eliciting their feedback regarding student participation and enthusiasm.

Reflection

- Students process the content during discussions with the group as they work to make the museum.
- Students write in their journals and complete "I learned" statements and group worksheets in which the groups evaluate their ability to work together.
- After each tour, the students and teacher discuss what went well and what they could do next time to improve their presentation skills.

SENIOR CENTER LUNCHEONS ■

Sometimes city schools have the advantage of not being very far from places that offer service-learning opportunities. One of our local elementary schools is only one block away from a senior citizens' center. Seniors gather there daily for companionship, activities, and lunch. The group of students who go to this senior center are chosen for various reasons. Some students need to feel more connected to school and some need to develop friends. Others are chosen because they are positive role models. The center offers wonderful learning opportunities for all of these students. The school counselor working with this group of students found that serving at the senior center was a great way to offer them an opportunity to develop social skills and important life skills at the same time.

Every Friday, this counselor walks with a group of students to the senior center. During this time, they review what they have learned about seniors and the challenges that they face. Prior to going to the senior center for the first time, the counselor conducted an activity where students get to experience what it feels like to have their vision and their movements obstructed. This type of activity is an example of Essential Element 10, which has to do with reflection prior to service. This activity, called the Empathy Activity, is described in the chart that follows.

When the students arrived at the center on their first visit, the kitchen staff explained the basics of food preparation. The students learned that hot food must be kept at a certain temperature and that cold food must be kept cold, and they observed the staff using thermometers to check for proper temperatures. The staff also explained food delivery to the students.

In their team-building activities and preliminary preparation, their counselor instructed the students on proper manners and appropriate ways to interact with the seniors. At the center, the students don plastic gloves and hairnets and set to work serving lunch to the seniors. When the students have finished delivering trays, they are expected to sit with the seniors and have conversations.

At special times—like Mother's Day, Father's Day, Halloween, Christmas, Easter, Passover, and Chanukah—the students often bring cards that they have made to the seniors. The seniors and the students often play games, and they have even completed a quilting project together. The students' work is hung

Figure 6.2   Serving Lunch

Used with permission of Sylena Drake, parent of Nhy'quan Drake, and Tonia L. Gardner, parent of Eric P. Gardner.

Name of Activity The Empathy Activity
Grade Level Elementary to middle school
Objectives To increase students' ability to work as members of a team To form positive relationships among students To increase students' empathy and understanding of others, especially senior citizens To provide opportunities for students to learn ways to assist an elderly person
Materials *Now One Foot, Now the Other* by Tomie depaola Props: puzzles, shirts on hangers, sunglasses with Vaseline™ on them, gardening gloves, ACE™ bandages, and Legos™

Procedure

Define empathy for the students; then read them the story *Now One Foot, Now the Other.* Discuss the story: How did Bobby and Bob's relationship change? Why was Bobby afraid of Bob? How do you think Bob felt when he came home from the hospital? Explain how Bobby was empathetic toward Bob.

Explain to students some of the conditions that residents at the nursing home might have (stroke, arthritis, cataracts, confusion). Have students learn what it feels like to have these afflictions by using the props: Place gloves on some students and have them try to play with Legos™ or button shirts. Place sunglasses with Vaseline™ on other students and have them do puzzles. Bind other students' fingers or hands with ACE™ bandages to simulate paralysis. During the activity, ask the students how it feels to try to complete the tasks with the challenge posed by physical obstacles. Have students try another prop and repeat the process of learning how it feels to try to do something with a physical obstacle in the way.

Discussion

Ask the students questions such as, What kinds of tasks that you do every day might be more difficult for a senior citizen? How could you help your friend at the senior center play bingo if they had cataracts or were hard of hearing? What are some other activities you might have to help another with?

around the center and is a great reminder of the wonderful collaboration that has taken place between two different generations.

After the service is completed, students reflect on it (see the questionnaire that follows). During reflection, students often reveal that they were initially afraid of the seniors. After going to the center a few times, they say that they are quite comfortable there. Because of their preparation activities and their firsthand experiences, the students have a better understanding of the challenges facing the elderly, including their loneliness, vision problems, chronic pain, hearing loss, and mobility problems. They also have learned useful life skills such as table manners, healthful food preparation, and social conversation.

Adaptation

As is always the case, a SERVICE-learning project can enhance academic subject content as well as personal development. In this project, students learn important information related to food service as well as appropriate social interaction with grown-ups. They also better understand the aging process and the challenges facing elderly people. Classroom teachers could integrate literature, writing, and social studies into this activity through specific assignments. Reading stories about elderly people, asking students to interview seniors and

Empathy Activity Reflection Sheet

Name _____   Date _____

Please respond to the following.

1. Define the word *empathy*.

2. How did you feel today when you needed help to do simple things?

3. How can what we learned today about empathy help you at the senior center?

4. Which of these problems—arthritis, cataracts, stroke, or confusion—is the most difficult in your opinion and why?

5. Do you know anyone in a nursing home, or do you have elderly relatives? If so, do they experience any of these problems?

6. Has your attitude toward them changed in any way?

7. What is the most important thing that you learned through this activity?

then write their stories, asking elders to tell the students what they remember about World War II, Korea, Vietnam, and the local history of their communities are just a few ideas for integrating content into service. Students could become advocates for issues facing the elderly, such as social security and Medicaid, by learning about the topics and writing to their local legislators. They would be learning important lessons about citizenship and government while advocating for their new friends.

Title of Service Experience

Senior Citizen Luncheons

Objectives

To increase students' awareness of issues related to aging

To increase students' empathy for the elderly

To strengthen students' connection to school through their social interactions with peers

To increase students' knowledge of safe food preparation and serving

To increase students' self-efficacy, confidence, and social competence

To increase students' citizenship and awareness of community resources

---

Learning Standards Supported by This Activity

English and language arts—reading; writing, listening, and speaking as social interactions

Career development and occupational studies—learning teamwork and cooperation, work experience

Health—learning about safe food preparation and service, proper hygiene

Social studies—learning about citizenship

Preparation Necessary for Program Implementation

- Contact a senior center to determine if they would like to partner with the school.
- Collaborate with the senior center activities director to prepare the seniors for the students' arrival. Explain the purpose of the program and what will be expected of the seniors.
- Develop a few activities to sensitize students to the elderly.
- Get permission for students to leave school for a period of time.

Preliminary Student Preparation

- Students need to do activities that will sensitize them to the needs of the elderly.
- Students need instruction in manners and to learn serving techniques.
- Students need to have their roles as servers and conversationalists explained to them.

Activity Summary

- Students go to the senior center once a week to serve lunch.
- Students put on plastic gloves and hairnets. They bring trays of food to the seniors, sit and talk with them as they eat, and then clear the table.
- Students may play games with the seniors or work with them on a project.

Assessment

Students' academic learning is not assessed in this example. However, if classroom teachers adapted this project, assessment of academic learning would relate to assignments such as interviews and written reports, advocacy letters, and so on. In this project, the counselor (or teacher) keeps close contact with the senior center manager and they work to ensure that both the seniors' and the students' needs are met. The level of satisfaction with the project has been good where it has been tried, and the seniors look forward to the students' visits.

Reflection

- On the walk back to school, students discuss their experiences.
- Once back at school, students complete questionnaires on which they write about their participation, how it made them feel, and what they learned.

■ FINAL WORDS

Service-learning is not magic. Not all subject content can be tied easily to service. Sometimes this strategy may not be an appropriate choice for a teacher who is working with students whose needs lie elsewhere. However, when educators know what outcomes they wish to achieve with their students, and why they are choosing service-learning as a strategy, service-learning can be effective. The examples you have just read are various forms of service-learning with huge potential for developing students' skills at two levels: the cognitive level and the social-emotional level.

It is important for teachers who are implementing service-learning to understand that there is preliminary work that needs to be done so that things will run smoothly and they will not be overwhelmed. As you read in Chapter 4, starting small and being prepared are two caveats that are well worth paying attention to. Depending on the age of the students, it is possible to enlist students to help with some of the initial preparation. Service-learning can be integrated into the school culture in many ways: through peer leadership groups, clubs, and afterschool programs, and, of course, through the curriculum. Creative teachers will find ways to adapt programs and connect subject matter to the act of service in order to enhance learning for students. Now, let's look at Chapter 7 and some more projects that you may find interesting.

Service-Learning Projects That Put Service First

You have not lived until you have done something for someone who can never repay you.

—Unknown

In Chapter 6 you read about five projects that could readily be adapted to the classroom setting in order to support curriculum tied to learning standards. In this chapter we will take a look at six more projects that may be adapted for classroom use, and where how to make such adaptations is not immediately apparent, I have added ideas for adaptation. These projects were designed to enhance students' personal development and civic involvement. Most of the students who were chosen for these programs needed to develop personal skills and attachment to school.

I urge you to look at these projects with an eye toward how you might reshape them and fit them to your own set of circumstances. Recall the discussion in Chapter 3 of designing service-learning projects with the end in mind. Consider what you wish to accomplish through the service-learning experience, and then shape your project accordingly. And remember to integrate into your project the Essential Elements of Effective Service-Learning in Chapter 3.

PEER TO PEER TRANSITION PROGRAM ■

Counselors at the elementary and middle school levels in a large suburban district initiated this program. The fourth graders in their district graduate from their small elementary schools and enter fifth grade in two large middle schools, accompanied by much trepidation and anxiety. The counselors decided to do something to ease these students' transition to middle school.

To start, they asked the fourth graders to help them make a list of what concerned them about entering middle school. They then took that list to the fifth graders, who were at that point veterans of middle school, and asked if they could think of any ways to help the fourth graders make the transition. The fifth graders gladly helped out. The result is a very successful program that has helped the fourth graders make the transition from elementary to middle school and the fifth graders become contributors to a positive school climate. Students from both grades reported that they enjoyed the experience. Fifth graders liked being "teachers" and being perceived as having knowledge and experience to share. Fourth graders reported being less anxious about entering a new building, and they liked the fact that they have already made a fifth grade pal. In addition, the fourth graders' parents reported feeling less anxious about their children's transition to middle school. This program could also work well for students moving from junior high to high school.

Although it was initiated by a small group of counselors, this program enlists all of the fourth and fifth grade teachers. It has evolved into an effort that begins in January and culminates in early June with a visit by the fourth graders to the middle school. The school district supports this program by providing busing for the students.

Teachers have seen the value of easing this transition and actively participate in the activities leading up to the visit. The fifth grade students work on their orientation program and are very prepared for the fourth graders when they arrive in June. The fourth graders' anxiety has been lessened and the fifth graders' self-efficacy has been increased, and that is what the program was designed to accomplish. However, as with all service-learning, much more learning happens than was initially anticipated. The following chart outlines the critical aspects of this project.

Title of Service-Learning Experience Peer to Peer Transition Program
Grade Level Elementary and middle school
Objectives • To ease elementary students' transition to middle school by lessening their anxiety • To foster relationships among students • To improve the overall middle school climate • To improve students' letter-writing ability • To increase middle school students' feelings of self-efficacy

Learning Standards Supported by This Activity

- *English and language arts*—writing, speaking, listening
- *Career development and occupational studies*—teamwork, cooperation, knowledge of systems
- *Social studies*—learning about citizenship, appreciation of rules and systems of governing

Preparation Necessary for Program Implementation

- Enlist the support of the elementary and middle school students' teachers. Communicate with them regarding the program logistics and timeline, such as when certain activities will take place and when things will be due.
- Create a form for parents' permission for the younger students' bus trip to the middle school.
- Create a description of the program for parents and teachers.
- Arrange busing between buildings for the meeting day at the end of the year.
- Arrange for elementary school students to have lunch with their middle school buddies.
- Create feedback forms to gather student, parent, and teacher input.

Preliminary Student Preparation

- Elementary school students are asked what questions, concerns, and worries they have about middle school, and middle school students are asked how they think they could assist the younger students.
- By January, with teacher assistance, elementary school students initiate pen pal letter writing between themselves and middle school students.
- With teacher assistance, elementary school students meet with middle school students to help the latter prepare their orientation program.

Activity Summary

This program starts in January and ends in early June, and it proceeds as follows:

- In January, teachers match elementary and middle school students, who start writing to each other. The students exchange letters periodically over the winter.
- The middle school students work on preparing an orientation day when the younger students will come to their building to get acquainted with them, the middle school routine, and the physical aspects of the building. They create learning stations that are staffed by middle school students and through which the younger students rotate during their visit.
- The younger students are greeted in a large group by the school's principal and given a quick "overview" of the middle school.

- The middle school students buddy up with their pen pals and take them through the stations. The younger students learn how to open lockers, what to expect for homework, what happens when you misbehave, where the nurse is, and so on.
- The visit ends with the older students giving the younger ones a tour of the building. The students eat lunch together.

Assessment

- Teachers assess the overall quality of the letters written and assign grades to the students.
- Students, teachers, and parents are asked for their feedback on this program to determine whether it made a difference in the students' transition to middle school.
- Elementary school students are asked to identify the rules and important information that they need to know in order to be successful in the new system of middle school. (This shows their understanding of the system.)
- Middle school students are asked to write about their experiences, including what parts of the project went well, what could be improved, and new ideas for next time.

Reflection

- Discussions take place with middle school students as they prepare their stations.
- Elementary school students reflect on the experience and how it makes them feel more prepared for the middle school.
- Middle school students reflect on their work and how it makes them feel.

■ DOLLS FOR KIDS PROJECT

This is a long-term project that engages students in making dolls for the pediatric unit of a local hospital. The teacher-adviser who developed this project was working with identified students in fourth to sixth grade in an inner-city school. It is a project that could be done with a group of identified students or with an entire classroom. It would be especially appropriate to connect it to home and careers curricula, or it could be part of a project connected with health. If students were reading books that had any connection to persons with illnesses or hospitals, it would be a great adjunct activity that would enhance the meaning of the literature.

Students learn how to trace and cut out simple two-piece doll patterns (see Figure 7.1). They cut out the material and sew the two pieces (front and back) together. The students learn to sew by sewing some parts of the doll with a machine and other parts by hand. They stuff the doll with soft material. Students then attach hair to the dolls' heads and draw or sew faces on the dolls. Voila! The dolls are ready to go to scared little children in the hospital. As noted in Chapter 2, conversation among students as they work is rich. They talk about illness, hospital stays, and what it must be like for the children in the hospital. They develop empathy as they hone fine motor and practical life skills.

Adaptation

Classroom teachers could devote a certain amount of time each week for work on the dolls. Kids would look forward to the hands-on action. In the meantime, assignments could revolve around the project. A math assignment could involve estimating how much material would be needed to make a certain number of dolls given that each doll takes .5 yards of material. Or the students could figure out how much stuffing would have to be purchased and

---

Name of Activity

Dolls for Kids Project

Grade Level

Elementary and middle school

Objectives

- To teach students to work cooperatively to complete a project
- To increase students' social interactions
- To increase students' self-esteem and self-efficacy
- To help students develop empathy for others
- To hone students' fine motor skills by sewing, pinning, and cutting
- To raise students' awareness of the health issues affecting children
- To teach students about hospitals, how they function, and who is hospitalized

---

Learning Standards Supported by This Project

English and language arts—writing, speaking, and listening as social interactions
Career development and occupational studies—teamwork, cooperation, knowledge of systems

Mathematics—using patterns, measuring

Home and careers—sewing

Health—awareness of diseases and hospital protocols

Preparation Necessary for Program Implementation

- Call a local hospital to inquire if there is an interest in the project. If so, set up a date when peer leaders can deliver the dolls.
- Prepare a list of local businesses (with addresses) from which to solicit donations of materials for the dolls.
- If appropriate, apply for grants from the PTA to fund the project.
- Write the procedure for making a doll for the students' reference.

Preliminary Student Preparation

- Discuss the purpose of the doll project, emphasizing empathy for hospitalized kids.
- Demonstrate the procedures of doll making.
- Demonstrate how to use a sewing machine.
- Demonstrate how to sew the dolls' faces and hair by hand using a needle and thread.

Activity Summary

- Students participate in a teacher-led discussion about the different reasons why children go to the hospital, how hospitals can be scary places for children, and how they can help by making dolls for patients to hug.
- Students design dolls, each drawing is voted on, and one is chosen. The doll design must be simple.
- Students receive handouts with the procedure for making a doll, and they brainstorm to come up with a list of the materials they'll need.
- Students write letters to local businesses to solicit donated materials. (Sometimes the PTA can help by donating some of the materials.)
- Students work on their doll patterns in small groups of two to three students. A simple doll design is drawn on a piece of cardboard. They trace the design and cut it out of construction paper, then pin the pattern to the material and cut it out.
- Students use their hands or the machines to sew the material together. They then turn the material inside out and stuff it, closing it with hand stitching. The students stitch on the dolls' hair and either draw or stitch on the dolls' faces.
- Each student writes a card to the patient who will receive the doll she or he has made.
- Students make a trip to the hospital to deliver the dolls to the nursing staff.

Assessment

If this project were done by a classroom teacher and integrated into curriculum, assessment would be related to assignments and could take the form of graded tests on material learned in math or health, written reports, or written reports of interviews with hospital staff.

Reflection

- Students reflect on this project through their participation in class discussions.
- Students could also be asked to keep a journal with their thoughts on the experience.
- Students are asked for feedback through completion of reflection sheets that ask students to talk about how they felt being a part of the project.

---

how much it would cost. Stories could be read about children who have survived childhood illnesses. Students could be asked to write about their own stories or make up one to write about, integrating what they have learned about how hospitals work.

Extra hands during the sewing times are essential. Parent and grandparent volunteers, high school students, and teachers' assistants are great helpers. Volunteers do not necessarily need to know how to sew. Hands are needed to thread needles, assist with pinning, and monitor the use of the sewing machines, if machines are available to use. It is best to work with small groups of two to three students while using machines. The more skilled students could help the ones who need more assistance. It is also best to have at least three sewing machines so that students can work on their own as much as possible. If an entire class is participating, some students could sew while others are engaged in other individual work.

When the dolls are completed, the students deliver them to the hospital. One nurse commented this year, "What a wonderful thing for the students to do. The dolls look absolutely beautiful, and I know the children will really like them." Teachers have seen very positive benefits for students who participate in this project. One wrote, "This has been great for D. The sewing has been great for her fine motor skills. The other students seem to be more patient with her in class."

MENTORING/TUTORING PROGRAM ■

This is a program run by a school counselor for selected students that connects junior high students with elementary students for the purpose of offering mentoring or tutoring to the younger students. If this project were adapted for high school students, they could connect with either junior high or elementary students. Students are chosen to participate based on interest, but students who

Figure 7.1   Making Dolls

Used with permission of Becky Rorick, parent of Cameron Rorick.

need to develop social skills, confidence, and connection to school are particularly encouraged to participate.

Students in this project meet throughout the year from October to May. They use their time together to reflect on their experiences and learn from one another. The junior high tutors and mentors have shown an improvement in their grades, self-esteem, self-awareness, and interpersonal skills. Through the experience of working with elementary students, the junior high students have gained powerful insights about themselves, as well as about the job of teaching. As with most forms of service-learning, the experience offers students self-knowledge as well as a glimpse into possible future career areas. Students in this program have made the following observations.

- "I learned that you have to be calm and loosen up when helping little kids."
- "I learned that I am kind and like meeting new kids."
- "I learned the responsibility of good behavior."
- "I didn't like that some of the kids didn't pay attention when we were trying to help them out." (Neither do I!)
- "I learned that I like taking care of kids."
- "Teaching can be fun!"

This project has the logistical challenge of trying to navigate two different systems in the same big system. Scheduling times for tutoring and mentoring can be difficult. Junior high and elementary schools' schedules are often very different. Lunch might start at 11:30 at one school and at 10:15 at the other. If you are lucky, sometimes schools have activity periods at the end of a day when this type of program can take place. Or, if lunchtimes at the schools are congruent, then using extended lunch periods for the program becomes an option.

There are many considerations in instituting a program like this. Junior and senior high school students' schedules always come first because their work is so time-consuming. They need to know what class will be missed and how they will make up the work. Transportation is always an issue—it has to be determined how the students will get to the elementary school if they cannot walk. And, of course, permission slips must be obtained from the students' parents. The preparation and scheduling for a project like this take time up front. Teachers must be invested and flexible. Principals must be supportive. Students must be committed so that younger kids are not disappointed by no-shows. As I mentioned in earlier chapters, once the groundwork has been laid and the program is up and running, the benefits far outweigh the work involved. The critical aspects of this project are in the following chart.

Title of Service Experience Mentoring/Tutoring Program
Grade Level Elementary to high school
Objectives Regarding Both Tutors and Tutees • To foster relationships among students • To give students a sense of school community and belonging • To improve students' school performance, behavior, and/or self-efficacy • To improve students' academic performance
Learning Standards Supported by This Activity • *English and language arts*—writing, speaking, listening • *Career development and occupational studies*—teamwork, cooperation, knowledge of systems • *Social studies*—learning about citizenship • Any other content area that students tutor in

Preparation Necessary for Program Implementation

- Enlist the support of K–8 teachers to identify students who need tutoring or mentoring and to identify students who would benefit from being tutors or mentors. Also, ask the teachers to be flexible in allowing students to make up class assignments if a class is missed.

- Create a form to obtain parents' permission for their children to participate.

- Create a description of the program for parents and school personnel.

- Arrange for the older students to have lunch in the elementary school if necessary.

- Create feedback forms for parents, teachers, and students.

- Collect the names of students who have volunteered or have been suggested by school personnel.

Preliminary Student Preparation

- Orient the older students to the procedures for both buildings (such as signing in and out, etc.).

- Discuss the appropriate behaviors students will be expected to model for the elementary students.

- Explain the consequences for positive and negative behaviors.

- Discuss the responsibilities, duties, and tasks of middle school students as tutors or mentors.

Activity Summary

- The older students select a time that they are free to go to the elementary school. This would be study hall or lunch.

- The older students may decide to eat lunch with the students they are tutoring.

- The older students may choose to help out a teacher in the classroom; help out a student with reading, vocabulary, artwork, or math in a one-on-one tutoring session; and/or deliver a lesson to the class.

- The older students are assigned tasks and responsibilities based on their own skill level.

- The older students walk over to the elementary school twice a week—on two days in a row or on alternate days, depending on the assigned activity.

- The older students are responsible for signing in and out of both buildings and for being on time for their next class.

Assessment

- Teachers monitor the grades, homework completion, and classroom behavior of students being tutored to determine if improvement has occurred.

- The counselor observes the older students and gets feedback from teachers and the older students themselves regarding their improvement in the areas of self-confidence, connection to school, grades, and behavior.

Reflection

- The schools' staffs meet with the students periodically to assess their work and get feedback from them on their feelings and their perceptions about the program.

- The students who were tutors or mentors write reflective statements on their experience.

HOW NOT TO FIGHT PROGRAM ■

This is a program that is currently taking place in a rural school setting. High school students teach a four-lesson curriculum to second graders on conflict management. How Not To Fight is produced by Sunburst Videos. The program is designed to positively affect school climate by teaching elementary students skills of conflict resolution. Originally, the school counselor intended to teach the curriculum. However, she and an elementary school counselor saw an opportunity to involve students in a great learning experience. They made the commitment to work together and the program was born. Now high school students teach the second graders, and they do it very effectively.

The high school students who teach this curriculum were trained in junior high to be peer mediators. Unfortunately, in their high school, there was little call for their skills. The students often felt discouraged that they were not being utilized in some way to improve the climate of the school. That is why the high school counselor decided to search out ways to use these positive peer leaders. Through this program, the peer leaders not only drew on previous training for this activity, they also developed new self-awareness and different skills.

As is usually the case, the providers of the service, namely the high school students, derive as much, or more, from the experience as do the second grade students. While the little ones learn important conflict resolution skills and thrive on the attention and novelty provided by the teens, the high school students learn about themselves and their abilities, interests, and challenges. Feedback from the high school students shows that they would like to go into the classes more often, and they would like to develop a follow-up lesson for the third grade. High school students stated that they feel more confident in themselves and that they like the experience of helping others.

Adaptation

This program focuses on the topic of conflict, but the topic could be anything that students are interested in and need to learn about. The act of teaching and the connection made between older and younger students is what is most important, and it could be made through any of a number of topics, such as making friends, resisting peer pressure, or substance abuse. As new high school students join this program, the other high school students could be used to train them or to take their places in this program when they move on. There are many possibilities for continuing this program.

In elementary schools, entire classrooms of students could learn the skills associated with the topic chosen and then buddy up with younger students to teach them the skills. Depending on the configuration of your school, the highest grade could teach any of the lower grades. The opportunity to teach could be a rite of passage for students who have made their way to the top of the school. I could envision sixth graders teaching third graders, and the third graders looking forward to the day when they would be the teachers. Not only would kids learn skills but the school climate would improve, positive role models would be created, and interpersonal and communication skills would be developed. The How Not To Fight Program is outlined in the chart below.

Title of Service Learning Experience   How Not To Fight Program
Grade Level   Elementary to high school
Objectives   • To increase younger students' knowledge of and skills in conflict resolution   • To increase older students' confidence and skills in public speaking and teaching   • To increase connection to school for all students involved   • To promote positive school climates
Learning Standards Supported by This Activity   *English and language arts*—speaking and listening as social interactions   *Social studies*—learning about citizenship

Health—promoting a safe environment, personal safety

Career development and occupational studies—career exploration

Preparation Necessary for Program Implementation

- Make scheduling arrangements for high school students to leave class.
- Arrange time periods for elementary students to participate in the program.
- Arrange for transportation between schools if necessary.
- Write a letter to parents asking permission for their high school students to walk to the elementary school.
- Write letters to the elementary students' parents informing them of the program and asking them to reinforce the content at home.
- Procure or make certificates and letters of congratulation for high school students to acknowledge their participation and to reinforce the positive nature of their work. (These can be used for their college applications.)

Preliminary Student Preparation

- Meet with high school students two to four times to explain teaching techniques and curriculum content.
- Assist high school students in developing lessons.
- Teach high school students classroom management techniques and appropriate ways to talk to elementary students.

Activity Summary

- High school students meet with advisers from both elementary school and high school to be coached in teaching the How Not To Fight curriculum. This may take two to four sessions.
- High school students meet in pairs four times with elementary school classes to teach the curriculum. They teach one class per week.
- Often older high school students are paired with younger high school students in order to help mentor them and share skills.

Assessment

- Elementary school teachers are asked to fill out a survey to determine if their students are using the skills of conflict resolution they were taught.
- Counselors assess the high school students' level of participation, commitment, and skill in teaching.

Reflection

- Informal conversations take place between advisers and high school students between classes. They discuss what went well and what could be improved.

- Counselors work with high school students to give them feedback on their performance and offer suggestions for improvement.

- The high school students reflect on the elementary students, on what they learned about teaching them and having to prepare lessons, as well as on their contribution to the elementary school climate and on what they learned about themselves.

- Teachers could also offer these students the opportunity to write about their experience for credit.

■ NURSING HOME VISITS

In one local suburban school district, the elementary school is only one block away from a nursing home. The school counselor decided to make a connection with the home as a way to begin a service-learning experience. She contacted the activities director and asked if she had any interest in establishing a relationship that would include students actually visiting the home and interacting with the elderly. The activities director was quite receptive, and soon they were working together to develop ideas.

The group that visits the home is considered a club. It meets during the activity period at the end of the day. The counselor invites the students who participate. She chooses students based on a variety of criteria. She looks for one or two students who will be positive role models for the others. She includes one or two students who are frequent visitors to the principal's office but who show leadership potential. She includes several students who show weak social skills. This year she included a student who exhibits frequent somatic complaints and who had a high rate of absenteeism. She may also invite students who are new to the school so that they can make friends.

All of the service-learning projects we have looked at thus far have two levels of outcomes. On one level, the activity increases students' knowledge and understanding, and on another level it produces personal development and change in students. The counselor who developed this program told me that the general objective for this activity was to provide an opportunity for students to develop intergenerational relationships and positive social skills. The more specific objectives include students' learning how to start and carry on a conversation with others, creating positive interactions with peers, and developing a heightened sense of self-esteem, empathy, and confidence.

The counselor who implements this program integrates times for the students to sit in a group and make something to bring to the seniors. They do this on days when they do not visit the home, since they visit only once per week. Cards or other artworks are created while the group talks with the counselor about the senior citizens and their special needs. They learn about the fact that seniors do not hear or see as well as younger people, and that they often need help moving around. They talk about what it is like for seniors to be old and no longer have their own homes. The counselor reinforces that the seniors' home is the nursing home now and they must take care to be respectful when they arrive. As they talk, they make gifts to bring to the home when they visit.

In activities like this one, you couldn't have predicted the wonderful things that students noticed when they visited. Students asked questions during the return walk to school like, "Why was that lady crying?" Or "Why was that man making those noises?" The counselor explained that sometimes elderly people miss their children or that they might have difficulty breathing. Students are naturally curious and they thrive on having an opportunity to ask thoughtful questions without being perceived as rude or insensitive. These questions indicated that the students were observing, caring, learning, and remembering. Parents appreciated the experiences their children were having, and some even related that they would take their children to visit their new elderly friends on their own time.

One of the most wonderful outcomes of this experience was that the students who were the most challenging in school were often terrific with the elderly. Teachers, not surprisingly, expressed surprise when they heard about how some of the more disruptive students behaved so well when they were at the home (like "Bobby" in Chapter 2). These students are compassionate and are not afraid to show the softer side of themselves when they are with the older people. The experience of working with the elderly gives students opportunities to gain insight into the needs of others and into disabilities. When they see the elderly people smile when they arrive, they realize that they have something important to offer others. As the counselor says, "They feel totally wanted there and recognize how much they brighten up the days of the individuals they visit."

One year, after meeting with the elementary students all year, the elderly decided that they would like to visit the school. Therefore, the last meeting of the year is now held at school where the children and seniors meet and celebrate. Some students perform for the seniors, and others show them their classrooms and their work. Students interview the seniors, asking questions about their school memories. Students then create booklets recording their interviews and adding artistic illustrations.

Students have learned many things from the seniors, like that in the old days kids took turns getting water from the well and that schools were much smaller. They were surprised that back then kids sometimes stayed in the same school from kindergarten to twelfth grade! For these students, learning seems so much more interesting when they are hearing about history firsthand.

The coordinator of this program related that at the end of last year an amazing thing happened. At the final visit of the year when the senior citizens came to school, the students put on a talent show and served goodies. One of the most popular boys in the group and another very shy boy who lacked social skills and confidence decided to do a duet for the talent show. The counselor

Figure 7.2   Nursing Home Visit

Used with permission of Bill Medina, parent of Elijah W. Medina.

said that it was wonderful to see these two young boys interact, clearly enjoying and respecting one another. She believes that if it weren't for this group, they would never have spoken a word between them because their social circles were so different. The experience of service-learning created a bond that will carry over into their normal school experience. The critical aspects of this project are in the chart that follows.

Title of Service Experience Nursing Home Visits
Grade Level Elementary school
Objectives • To foster relationships among students • To give students a sense of community and belonging

- To improve students' school performance, behavior, and/or self-esteem
- To offer students an opportunity to develop intergenerational relationships

Learning Standards Supported by This Activity

- *English and language arts*—writing, speaking, listening
- *Career development and occupational studies*—teamwork, cooperation, knowledge of systems
- *Social studies*—learning about citizenship

Preparation Necessary for Program Implementation

- Locate a nursing home and activities director who will work with the school.
- Enlist the support of teachers who will refer students for the program.
- Acquire parental permission for students to participate.
- Arrange for transportation if necessary.
- Plan activities that students can do with the elderly and the times for students' visits.
- Make craft materials available for students to make cards and items to bring to the elderly.

Preliminary Student Preparation

- Review the conduct expected of students during the trip to the nursing home and while they are there.
- Discuss what a nursing home is and what to expect.
- Remind them that it is the residents' home and that students need to be respectful.
- Discuss how students should walk near the elderly so as not to harm them.
- Discuss the other needs of the residents.

Activity Summary

- Students walk (or are bused) to the nursing home.
- Students assist residents during their activity time and join in their activities.
- Students interview seniors about their own school experiences and then create booklets that record and illustrate the information.
- Once per year, the seniors visit the school.

Assessment

This activity is not directly related to any academic learning objectives. However, the interviews that the students do and the booklets they create could be considered part of English and language arts and considered for a grade. The coordinator maintains close contact with the nursing home director to make sure that the level of satisfaction with the program and students' conduct is satisfactory.

Reflection

- Students meet during their lunch periods to discuss and process the visit and make plans for future visits.
- Students could also write in journals or write essays about their experience.

■ HELMET SAFETY PROGRAM

This program is done in a very large suburban middle school. The students who participate in this program are chosen carefully. Students who exhibit the need for social skill development, behavior management, confidence, and/or school connection are invited to participate.

This program was started after the death of a middle school student when the bicycle he was riding was hit by a car. He was not wearing a helmet at the time. Twice since his death 4 years ago, students have implemented and dedicated this program to the young boy who lost his life. The program gives students the opportunity to learn about helmet safety, to purchase a discounted helmet, and to have their helmets properly fitted.

The teacher-adviser who created this program invites professionals from the county Safety Council to come to school and teach all of the sixth grade classes about bicycle and helmet safety. Afterward, the students who are participating in the service-learning program get a lesson on helping others to properly fit their helmets. These trained sixth grade students visit classes to make presentations on helmet safety, and they invite fellow fifth and sixth grade students to bring their helmets to school to be fitted properly. If anyone does not own a helmet, an opportunity to purchase a helmet at a very reduced cost is offered. The teacher-adviser of this program also collaborates with a very popular restaurant to provide incentives for the students if they participate. Students receive a gift certificate and tokens if they participate in the program.

The 36 students who participated in this service-learning program last year knew that they were doing very important work. They were given responsibility for creating flyers advertising the program, for speaking to classes, and for actually fitting helmets on students' heads. As one student said, "I may have saved a life. I realize the importance of helmet safety." Another added, "It felt great to teach the younger kids. They really listened!" This program has been quite successful. Last year 420 students either had a helmet fitted or purchased a new one.

Title of Service Experience

Helmet Safety Program

Grade Level

Middle school

Objectives

- To increase students' social skills and self-confidence
- To foster positive relationships among students
- To increase students' knowledge of bicycle and helmet safety
- To increase students' feelings of self-efficacy

Learning Standards Supported by This Activity

English and language arts—listening, reading, speaking

Health—learning about personal safety

Social studies—learning about civic responsibility

Preparation Necessary for Program Implementation

- Contact the local safety council to schedule a speaker for an assembly program.
- Schedule additional training for the service-learning group.
- Contact local restaurants or merchants and ask them to make donations that will serve as incentives for participation.
- Schedule presentations by students to classes.

Preliminary Student Preparation

- Students need to learn how to fit helmets.
- Students need to learn how to present information to classes.

Activity Summary

- All classes get trained on helmet safety by professionals.
- Students get trained to fit helmets.
- Students create flyers to advertise the program.
- Students create a form for those who wish to purchase a new helmet.
- Students make a presentation to other classes and encourage students to bring in a helmet or purchase a new one for a reduced rate.
- Students visit classes and fit helmets on students.

Assessment

- The desired outcomes for this project have to do with students' personal and social development, and so surveys are given to teachers to determine if they have observed any positive behavioral changes in the students who participated. (See the sample form that follows.)
- Students are asked to fill out an assessment of their own perception of their growth.

Reflection

- Students reflect on their experience in discussions during the activity.
- Students each fill out a questionnaire regarding the experience, and they discuss their responses as a group.

Service-learning that focuses on service usually has increasing students' social and personal skills as the primary objectives. The feedback form below can be adapted to any individual program and then given to teachers or others who know the students to help determine the effectiveness of the program and whether the desired outcomes for students' personal development have been achieved. Program assessment also ought to include students' opinions of their own level of learning and improvement (see the questions and questionnaire for students in Chapter 5 on pages 69 and 70).

Service-Learning Teacher Pre-Post Assessment

Please fill out this form before and after the service-learning experience.

Date _____

Student _____ Teacher _____

This student is going to be participating in my service-learning group for the next _____ weeks. The group will be involved in many activities designed to give the students opportunities for meaningful contribution. They will be learning important life skills that we hope will have a positive impact on their school lives.

Please take a few moments to help me determine the areas in which this student needs to improve (and later if improvement has been noted).

Pre		Post
	This student shows	
_____	Leadership ability but not necessarily in positive ways	_____
_____	Difficulty in making or keeping friends	_____
_____	Difficulty with academic achievement or interest	_____
_____	Lack of self-confidence	_____
_____	Behavior problems such as _____	_____
_____	Anxiety	_____
_____	Shyness	_____
_____	Low attachment to school	_____
_____	Low attachment to community	_____
_____	Difficulty dealing with adults	_____
_____	Other _____	_____

FINAL WORDS ■

As discussed throughout this book, there are many ways to use the strategy of service-learning to increase students' academic and personal learning. The examples given in Chapters 6 and 7 offer just a few. I purposely took examples from actual programs I am familiar with rather than using examples from other books or the Internet. (See the Resources section of this book for many places to gather project ideas.)

In reading about the programs described here, you can see the thinking that occurred prior to the creation of the project and what objectives drove the focus of the project. These projects were created by people who were not trained in service-learning. In fact, as I observed these projects and recorded the information about how they were developed and implemented, I was able to identify connections to curriculum and standards that the creators did not intend. They were, of course, thrilled that their projects were accomplishing so much more than they initially intended. These projects would have been even more effective had the creators known about and integrated the Essential Elements of Effective Service-Learning. As you adapt one of these projects, revisit

Chapter 3 and make sure that your project has incorporated the elements to ensure that you are creating high-quality service-learning experiences for your deserving students.

Now that we have looked at the logistics of developing programs, Chapter 8 focuses on sustaining service-learning efforts.

8

Sustaining Service-Learning Efforts

Let us put our minds together and see what life we can make for our children.

—Tatanka Iyotak (Sitting Bull)

As the movement toward higher educational standards takes hold, administrators are increasingly being held accountable for the achievement of their students. Schools and districts are often compared to one another, and administrators are under pressure to make sure that their students and staffs perform well. As a result, many administrators may be reluctant to embrace service-learning because it is a strategy that is nontraditional and still somewhat new. Historically, education is slow to adapt to new pedagogies, even though they may support recent information about how the brain learns and how students are motivated and engaged.

Service-learning has been shown to increase students' academic achievement, connection to school, and self-efficacy; foster bonds between school and community; and develop students' personal traits, such as character, responsibility, and empathy. No administrator needs to be convinced that these outcomes are desirable. However, the administrator's job is to ask the tough questions and to make sure that all bases are covered when it comes to standards, curriculum, and assessment. Administrators are the ones who must answer to parents, school boards, and community members. Their reluctance to jump on bandwagons is understandable and admirable. Fortunately, service-learning is an approach with a growing research base that has shown amazing results. Clearly it is worthy of an administrator's support and commitment.

This chapter gathers the many benefits of service-learning discussed in this book so that what is of interest to administrators can be found in one place. Knowing that administrators are busy people, I have tried to make it easy to access information that is pertinent to administrators and their broad concerns.

■ ADMINISTRATORS HOLD THE KEYS

According to the Education Commission of the States (ECS), superintendents and principals are integral to clearing the path so that the essential elements of quality service-learning can be initiated and sustained (ECS, 2000). Schools that wish to begin or improve their service-learning efforts, and ensure that service-learning is of the highest quality possible, must start at the top. Making service-learning a part of the mission of a district or mentioning service-learning in one of the district's strategic goals ensures that it is part of the school culture.

Leadership is key to every innovation, and one fine example of leadership is the actions taken by Dr. Sheldon Berman of Hudson, Massachusetts. His actions are strongly supported by the research of Elmore (1996), who suggests that the following four things are necessary for programs to be sustained:

1. Strong norms for practice

2. Cultures or policies that encourage challenging practice

3. Intentional strategies that allow reproduction of successes

4. Professional development that fosters new learning and incentives to support it

With Berman's strong direction, a Community Service-Learning Leadership Team was instituted in his district. This team planned programs, secured grants, developed an inservice packet for each teacher, and provided planning and oversight for service-learning efforts in the district. After the teams generated support from the schools for service-learning, Berman helped to build continuity among schools and grade levels by expecting that all principals request that their teachers find a way to integrate service-learning into their classrooms whenever possible. In addition, he worked with his school board to garner members' support. As a result of his leadership and the efforts of his principals and their staffs, service-learning is integrated into the curriculum districtwide (ECS, 2000).

In the Hudson School District, students at each grade level have an opportunity to participate in service-learning of some kind. Kindergartners have four projects they participate in, including a quilting program. First graders collaborate with a senior citizen center. Second and third graders collaborate with a local food pantry. Fourth graders work on a year-long environmental preservation project in the wetlands and forests. Fifth graders works with reading buddies. Environmental science classes work on projects surrounding the local river. Social justice classes work on a project dealing with hunger. Virtually all grade levels are involved in some type of project that helps students develop citizenship skills. According to Berman, the district has worked hard to ensure that all the projects are integrated into the curriculum. Their high school has been reorganized into thematic clusters. As a result, teachers can work together with students to integrate service-learning into the school experience. This school has made service-learning a priority and, with sound leadership, has provided the necessary resources to sustain efforts. Without that support, this type of progress would be difficult to achieve and maintain.

Billig and Klute (2002) studied grantees of the W. K. Kellogg Foundation between 1990 and 1999. A list of what the grantees learned about sustainability follows:

1. It takes different skills and messages to envision and stimulate the adoption and implementation of service-learning than to sustain service-learning.

2. It is necessary to develop and nurture long-term community partnerships if institutionalization of service-learning is to be achieved.

3. It is important to start working on sustainability at the beginning of a service-learning project.

4. Institutionalization of service-learning is more likely when there are funds to support a paid staff person.

5. Institutionalization is more likely when the project has tangible, positive results and when those involved in it are engaged in continuously improving the project.

6. Institutionalization is more likely when service-learning is directly connected to educational reform.

7. When support from leaders and advisory boards is maintained, sustainability is more likely.

IMPORTANT QUESTIONS TO CONSIDER ■

Liability

There are often questions regarding liability when considering service-learning within the community. Boards of education are interested in the issue of liability for obvious reasons. Money is scarce enough without adding to the problem by instituting a program that could at some point lead to a lawsuit. Since laws differ from state to state, it is advisable to contact your school district's counsel for information and advice on this issue.

Service-learning is really no different from other field trip experiences. The same rules apply, and the keys to successful experiences are preparation and having enough quality supervision of students by staff. Here are some important things to remember:

- Be sure to always have all parents' signed permission slips. The slips should specify *where* their child will be going, the *length of the time* the child will be away from school, and the *mode of transportation.*
- If a student or staff member is injured while on site, the school district is responsible, just as they are when staff and students are at school.
- If a traffic accident occurs during transit, the school district is responsible. If a private company is providing transportation, they bear responsibility. However, school districts are likely to be involved as well if litigation results from the accident.

- Be sure to have a *safe ratio* of staff to students for proper supervision.
- Be sure to have a *plan* in place in the event that a student or staff person becomes ill while at the service site (that is, alternative transportation back to school).
- Be sure develop policies, procedures, and job descriptions. Make sure that those who might need them have emergency phone numbers. Address safety concerns.
- Taking care to prepare for any anticipated problems will assure administrators, boards of education, and parents that this experience is well managed.
- Provide a list of all places that students will be going in the community to the district business office so that they have that information for the insurance company.
- Consult your district's business official to make sure the district insurance covers the service-learning program you plan to implement (Anderson & Witmer, 2002).

Administrative Concerns

The Education Commission of the States issued a paper on service-learning and community service in May of 2000. In it, they discussed the important role that administrators have in supporting and strengthening service-learning in their schools. The paper was based on conversations with teachers and administrators who have discovered and are now committed to service-learning. According to the ECS paper, there are important questions that inquisitive administrators may wish to address as they consider instituting or supporting this strategy. Teachers may also be interested in the answers to these questions since they are the ones most likely to be affected by the approach. The questions are as follows:

Does service-learning conflict with course content?

On the contrary, service-learning can make course content come alive by connecting content with real-world issues within the community. Students have the opportunity to apply their learning in practical ways and, as a result, engage higher-order thinking skills. When they have an opportunity to participate in meaningful ways, they engage more actively in their course content and learn at a deeper level.

In order to adopt service-learning as a practice, teachers need administrative support and encouragement to look for ways of connecting their curriculum to service opportunities. The study of science is ripe with opportunities for students. Working at nature centers, planting gardens, and cleaning up parks and streams are but a few ways that science can leave the classroom and connect to the outside world. Social studies and civics are also loaded with possibilities, from interviewing veterans of wars to serving at soup kitchens. Experiences like these make learning about the causes of the Vietnam War or the economics of the Great Depression much more meaningful for students.

Is it fair to ask already burdened teachers to begin incorporating service-learning?

As the ESC paper (2000) indicates, teachers will initially need staff development to learn the basics of the service-learning technique. However, they will soon see the benefits in more engaged students and more exciting learning. The investment of teacher time will lessen once teachers have completed their preparations by establishing community connections and working out the logistics of the service-learning. As ECS put it, "Many teachers believe that students get so much mileage from service-learning that it is well worth the investment of time and energy" (ECS, 2000, p. 5). Usually, a few interested teachers get the service-learning ball rolling, and then others learn from their achievements, as well as their mistakes. There is nothing like positive role modeling to inspire others to try new ideas.

Is it OK to require students to do volunteer work?

It is important to remember that service-learning is not volunteer service. Some administrators fear coming under fire from parents because they think that the school is requiring community service. ECS (2000) reminds us that "service-learning is not a volunteer activity at all, but a deliberate educational strategy designed to help schools accomplish two of their primary missions, teaching students to high standards and preparing them to be competent citizens" (p. 5).

Does service-learning take more time than regular teaching?

The most honest answer to this question is, "Initially, yes, but not forever." In fact, anytime you do something for the first time, it takes more time. Remember writing your first lesson plan? There is always a learning curve no matter how important or how mundane the task. As time goes on, service-learning tasks become routine, relationships become established, and projects are less time-consuming. Teachers find that the extra effort is well worth the time spent early on. There are a few key ideas to remember here, which are listed below.

• High-quality service-learning is connected to curriculum and standards. Therefore, teachers must put some thought into their intended service experience. They must determine ways that service can be woven into curriculum content so that students engage, learn, and develop deeper understanding as a result of their service experience.

• Not all service-learning is the same. Some teachers may choose to integrate into the curriculum indirect service projects, such as collecting money for cancer or diabetes foundations when students are studying those topics in health classes. Others may connect a piece of literature to a service project. Research shows, however, that service-learning is more powerful when students have direct contact with people in the settings in which they serve (Billig, 2004). Serving the homeless, tutoring younger students, planting gardens, and working with elderly people have more impact than doing projects on others' behalf. However, the value of indirect service is clear. Even indirect service and advocacy enhance learning and engage students.

- Teachers who choose to venture into the community to develop relationships with agencies in order to provide service will initially have extra work because they will need to research service sites and meet with the people who will help arrange the service-learning opportunities. For example, it is time-consuming to contact nursing homes or daycare centers to arrange for visits and jobs for students to do. Once done, however, such jobs can roll on for years, as long as all parties are satisfied. (This may be a great area in which to engage willing parents. They could contribute by taking on some of the legwork and research associated with initiating community contacts. They may even work at places where students could serve.)

- Teachers, in collaboration with counselors, older students, parent volunteers, or aids, may develop projects and connect the projects to the curriculum and standards. Students from about sixth grade on should be able to review the standards that they are responsible for learning. They should also be able to think of service-learning project ideas.

If someone other than the teacher assists in implementing the service-learning project, it is necessary that high levels of communication between the teacher and that person be maintained. It is also imperative that the teacher participates in the reflective process to ensure that the students make appropriate connections and that higher-order thinking is stimulated. Teachers might consider developing English and language arts assessment questions related to the service-learning of their students.

Teachers have found that the additional work involved with service-learning abates as time goes on: "Particularly as teachers gave increasing responsibility for planning, action, reflection, and assessment to the students, they found that students began to take more ownership, learn more, and become more responsible" (RMC Research Corporation, 2003, p. 2).

■ WHAT DO ADMINISTRATORS NEED TO KNOW AND DO?

Administrators can do a great deal to help promote, support, and sustain service-learning. Without supervisory support and encouragement, teachers are unlikely to try something new, let alone garner enough energy to sustain their efforts. I have known many teachers who have gotten bogged down in their own routines because their administrators lacked enthusiasm and leadership skills. One of the most effective ways for administrators to show teachers, students, and parents that they are committed to an idea or approach is to make it part of the mission and create policies to support it. That way, because teachers' involvement in service-learning is part of their working toward the school's mission, they know that their efforts will not go unnoticed or unappreciated.

It is imperative that administrators provide leadership. ECS (2000) outlines the type of leadership that is necessary to sustain service-learning. They suggest that administrators take the important steps outlined below.

Provide Leadership

Begin with including service-learning in vision, mission, goals, and strategies. Garner support for service-learning from school boards and community officials. Allow flexibility in scheduling to provide for sufficient time to complete projects. Find connections between service-learning and other programs offered in the district. Find ways for students to present their work and accomplishments.

Allocate Time, Money, and Other Resources

Create an infrastructure to support service-learning—possibly hire a coordinator or offer minigrants to staff and provide time and grant-writing expertise to find money for activities. Offer transportation to and from sites. Provide service-learning reference and resource kits for teachers and interested staff. Help teachers connect service-learning to the curriculum. Since most teachers are asked to do additional duties, such as cafeteria or bus duty, consider making service-learning an option for teachers' additional duty and relieve them of another one.

Develop and Support Teachers

Establish committees and create systems of support and staff development. Use curriculum coordination meetings to build consistency among grades. Make sure service-learning adheres to the Essential Elements of Effective Service-Learning. Provide mentoring and study groups for implementing service-learning and inservice for new teachers. Recognize service-learning projects.

Work With State Leaders

It is important that state leaders understand what is happening in the area of service-learning. Keep them informed by recognizing and publicizing outstanding projects. Invite them to your schools to see for themselves.

Build Partnerships

Work with local businesses, agencies, and colleges to establish relationships and attract projects. Keep parents informed and elicit their support.

Recognize and Celebrate

Identify and recognize important leaders in the service-learning field. Make sure newspapers and district communications people are aware of service-learning projects and are bringing that information to the public. Give awards publicly and provide opportunities for students to make presentations.

FINAL WORDS ■

Myriad issues fly across administrators' desks daily, even hourly. It is no wonder that administrators are not looking for more things to do. Why, they may ask, would they want to initiate service-learning projects when standards and assessments have become so critical and time-consuming? If service-learning is not required, why add it to the mix? One reason is that service-learning actually is a vehicle that has the ability to take them where they want to go. As Terry Pickeral, director of the Compact for Learning and Citizenship, said, "Service-learning has the potential to create safe schools, reconnect the public to public education, address academic learning outcomes, develop a new generation of citizens and re-ignite the spirit in each classroom teacher" (ECS, 2000).

School administrators are concerned with academic excellence, student development, and school-community relations. Service-learning enhances an administrator's ability to positively affect all three of these areas. Students want and need to be engaged in active learning, and service-learning can provide that activity. Effective service-learning is aligned with state or district standards, making it an enhancement to classroom instruction. Service-learning also assists young people in developing character and values, and service-learning is a good vehicle for schools in interacting with the community in positive, proactive ways. Finally, quality service-learning can only be sustained if it has the support from administrators and governing boards of education.

Service-Learning: What, So What, and Now What?

I learned that it's very important to help every chance you get. When I did this I felt important and needed, also that I am very lucky to have everything I have. I feel very sad about the people who don't have everything I do, and I am glad I could help.

—Fourth grade participant in a holiday giving project

WHAT ABOUT SERVICE-LEARNING? ■

My old friend Mary Poppins once sang a song about a spoonful of sugar helping medicine go down. For many students, school is a lot like medicine. They know it is good for them, but they do not want to take it. However, if they are involved in service-learning, for at least part of their school time, typical students may find their needs for excitement, novelty, and movement met. When students get to learn through service projects that they have had a voice in developing, taking the school medicine is not so terrible. They may even come to see how good it is for them and look forward to it. It is amazing how students can tolerate the difficult parts of school, like behaving and doing challenging class work, when they know that something they value awaits them.

I began this book with students' voices, and I have tried to include their voices within the text. Most of the voices you have heard belong to youngsters who have experienced an opportunity to give to someone else, sometimes for the first time. If you listen to their words, they almost always talk about how good it makes them feel to do something important for another. They often talk about insights that they have gained about themselves, their personalities, their abilities, their fears, and their hopes. They have learned to work as teams through their projects and to appreciate people's differences.

As you have read, service-learning has positive effects on the hard-to-engage student. The research is confirming this. However, we should not forget that quality service-learning that is connected to curriculum, of sufficient duration, and incorporates the Essential Elements of Effective Service-Learning also has the power to engage and challenge the already engaged student. Please listen to the voice of one such student, Stephen DeSalvo.

> When my sixth grade teacher, Ms. S., introduced a contest to help kids with bullying, she introduced doing something that would be a service-learning project, and fun for me! First I made a basic web site with the definition of a bully and why it's not right to bully. Then people from my class told me to start adding things like an advice column and defining other words people who are dealing with bullying might want to know. As the web site grew and grew, we decided to make the web site something that the school and community could call its own, to help kids with bullying. I went to classrooms with my peers and presented it to fifth and sixth graders and they were excited to know that they have somewhere to go, and [they] still do!
>
> People all over the country can view this web site (http://sdesalvo9.tripod.com/respect). On this web site, we offer the definition of a bully . . . words to know . . . types of respect and a questions and answers section. In the questions and answers section, kids can get advice from their peers on what they should do. The best part is, everything is confidential. The person being bullied will e-mail an address to state the problem on an address that everyone can use. . . . A group of 2 or 3 peers then come up with a solution to the [problem] and post it for everyone to see on the web.
>
> This web site makes me feel like I made a difference, that I helped someone and everyone with what may seem to them a never ending problem. I have experienced being bullied before myself, and almost everyone has. At this web site though, your solutions can be found. I know that the other kids who helped answer questions also feel great, that they also made a difference. I think that everyone should have the chance to feel that way, and they can! Service learning is a great way to help others, and the best part is that kids can help other kids.

Throughout this book, I have cited research that supports the use of service-learning as an educational strategy. Yet two noted researchers, Billig and Furco (2002), tell us that there is a great need for additional solid K–12 research on the academic, civic, and personal benefits of service-learning. There is a need for more solid evidence of the effectiveness of service-learning if this pedagogy is to become embedded into curricula and instruction.

The projects that I have presented have not been formally studied for effectiveness, and yet teachers and others involved would testify to their positive benefits for students. These projects were already up and running when I began to write this book, and in analyzing them I found that most had incorporated the four main aspects of service-learning: preparation, implementation, reflection, and celebration. Sometimes good old intuition can get things started, and the research that confirms common sense follows.

I believe that this book has provided a base from which interested teachers and other educators can begin service-learning efforts. Ideas for projects have been presented, along with guidance on the logistical preparation necessary prior to the service-learning experience. The Essential Elements have been offered as a guide to planning, development, and implementation of service-learning projects.

SO WHAT? ■

Educators all over the country struggle with test results. In my own state of New York, many hours are devoted to discussion about what the data indicate about instruction and learning. Educators analyze dips in scores, trying to create explanations that might lead to insights that will result in higher test scores next time.

One thing we might do is pay attention to *how* we teach more than *what* we teach. We need to recognize that, more than anything else, children, and especially adolescents, need to be in relationships. They want to be in relationships with their peers, of course, but they also want and need to be in relationships with their teachers and other caring adults. They need to know that they are valued for their abilities, whether those abilities are related to their schoolwork or not. They need to know that we care about them and that we like them. Service-learning is one way to build relationships with students as they learn.

The Search Institute's most recent survey (1999–2000) revealed that only 29% of the over 217,000 students surveyed in Grades 6 to 12 perceived that their schools offered caring environments (Search Institute, n.d.). Kids need to know that we care, and we need to learn better ways to show them. We need to listen to the experts who are informing the field of education. Kathy Checkley (2004) quotes Pat Wolfe, who writes extensively on how the brain learns, as having said that "adolescence is not a time to sit and take notes." Wolfe urges teachers to harness the passion of the adolescent. Young people are passionate about everything, especially their friends and their ideas. Wolfe tells us to take that energy and use it. I couldn't agree more. We can show our kids that we care by teaching them in ways that engage them, their interests, and their positive attributes. Service-learning is one very effective way to do this.

NOW WHAT? ■

Now I urge you to take some time to reflect on all that you have just read. I suggest that you find like-minded people in your school and talk about what you can do to make your instruction more exciting and more connected to the real world. Think of a project idea that could relate to more than one subject area and enlist another teacher to plan with you. Revisit Chapter 3 and review the

Essential Elements of Effective Service-Learning to make sure you plan a project that will be of high quality. Look again at Chapter 4 to review what has to be done to lay the groundwork for quality service-learning experiences.

Remember that service-learning is most likely to be successful with an organizational culture of support, with sufficient development of staff to respond to students' needs, with projects starting small and growing slowly, and with those responsible paying attention to quality (Billig & Klute, 2002).

Once you have had a successful experience with service-learning, you will most likely become an advocate for this instructional strategy. Your students may engage in ways that you have not seen before, and you will feel more effective and energized than ever. Now, I wish you much success and continued good teaching.

Resources

Resources on State Policies

Education Commission of the States (ECS). (2001). ECS state notes. *Service-learning policy scan: Institutionalized service-learning in the 50 states, March 2001.* Retrieved February 22, 2005, from www.ecs.org/nclc

RMC Research Corporation. (2002). *Policy, K–12 service-learning.* Retrieved May 24, 2004, from www.servicelearning.org/article/archive/123

Resource on Federal Legislation and Service-Learning

Billig, S., & Brown, S. (2002). *Opportunities for service-learning in the No Child Left Behind Act of 2001.* Retrieved April 25, 2005, from www.servicelearning.org/resources/online-documents/the_2001_no_child_ left_behind_act/

Resource on Social and Emotional Learning

Collaboration for Social, Academic, and Emotional Learning. (2000). *Making the case for social and emotional learning and service-learning.* Retrieved April 25, 2005, from www.ecs.org/clearinghouse/44/04/4404.pdf

Useful Web Sites

www.closeup.org/servlern.htm is the Web site of the Close Up Foundation's *Service Learning Quarterly,* a resource for educators that offers project plans that incorporate service into standards-based curriculum. The disciplines addressed by the projects include English, social studies, history, science, and art. Additional project plans are included in each issue.

www.cns.gov is the Web site of the Corporation for National and Community Service, a federal government site that seeks to involve people of all ages and backgrounds in service to their communities.

www.dropoutprevention.org is the Web site of the National Dropout Prevention Center/Network. It offers a link to service-learning and its benefits for "at risk" students.

www.kidsconsortium.org is the Web site of the Kids Consortium, an organization working with teachers, administrators, and students to promote learning through community involvement.

www.mssa.sailorsite.net/best.html is the Web site of the Maryland Student Service Alliance, which offers simple and practical information regarding service-learning as well as summaries of actual projects. The site also provides a useful service-learning project evaluation form in "Maryland's Best Practices: An Improvement Guide for School-Based Service-Learning."

www.nslexchange.org is the Web site of the National Service-Learning Exchange, which supports high-quality service-learning programs in schools, colleges and universities, and community organizations.

www.nwrel.org/learns/index.html is the Web site of the Linking Education and America Reads through National Service (LEARNS), a partnership of Northwest Regional Educational Laboratory, Southern Regional Council, and Bank Street College of Education. LEARNS provides training and technical assistance for projects focusing on literacy and education.

www.nwrel.org/ruraled/learnserve/index.html is the Web site of the Northwest Regional Laboratory's Learn and Service Project site. The site provides information, highlights rural schools with service-learning programs, and provides links to local and national service-learning resources.

www.nylc.org is the Web site of the National Youth Leadership Council (NYLC), whose mission is to engage young people in their communities and schools through innovation in learning, service, leadership, and public policy. NYLC is at the forefront of educational reform efforts.

www.projectserviceleadership.org is the Web site of the Project Service Leadership, an organization committed to improving the quality of our schools and communities by tapping the talents and energy of youth.

www.rmcdenver.com is the Web site of the RMC Research Corporation that offers current research on service-learning, including essential elements and benefits.

www.servicelearning.org is the Web site of the National Service-Learning Clearinghouse, which supports service-learning in higher education, in kindergarten through twelfth grade, in community-based initiatives, and in tribal programs. They assist with materials, references, referrals, and information. The center of the clearinghouse is at the University of Minnesota.

References

Anderson, C. S., & Witmer, J. T. (2002). *Addressing school board and administrative concerns about service-learning.* Retrieved April 26, 2005, from www.lions quest.org/content/resources/servicelearningarticles/slarticle15.htm

Billig, S. (2000). Research on K–12 school-based service-learning: The evidence builds. *Phi Delta Kappan, 81*(9), 658–663.

Billig, S. (2004). Research matters. *Talk It Up: Advocating for Service-Learning, 8.* Retrieved April 30, 2004, from www.service-learningpartnership.org

Billig, S., & Conrad, J. (1997). *Annual report: K–12 service-learning and educational reform in New Hampshire.* Denver, CO: RMC Research Corporation.

Billig, S., & Furco, A. (2002). Research agenda for K–12 service-learning: A proposal to the field. In A. Furco & S. Billig (Eds.), *Service-learning: The essence of the pedagogy.* Greenwich, CT: Information Age.

Billig, S., & Klute, M. (2002). *W. K. Kellogg Foundation retrospective of K–12 service-learning projects, 1999–2000.* Denver, CO: RMC Research Corporation.

Boston, B. (1997). *Service-learning: What it offers to students, schools, and communities.* Washington, DC: Council of Chief State School Officers.

Bransford, J. D. (1993). Who ya gonna call? Thoughts about teaching problem solving. In P. Hallinger, K. Leithwood, & J. Murphy (Eds.), *Cognitive perspectives on educational leadership.* New York: Teachers College Press.

Carrera, M. (1999). *Lessons for lifeguards.* New York: Donkey Press.

Checkley, K. (2004, August). Meeting the needs of the adolescent learner. *Education Update, 46*(5), 8.

Conrad, D., & Hedin, D. (1991, June). School-based community service: What we know from research and theory. *Phi Delta Kappan, 72*(10), 743–749.

Covey, S. (1990). *The 7 habits of highly effective people.* New York: Free Press.

Dewey, J. (1916). *Democracy and education.* New York: Free Press.

Duckenfield, M., & Swanson, L. (1992). *Service learning: Meeting the needs of youth at risk.* Clemson, SC: National Dropout Prevention Center.

Duckenfield, M., & Wright, J. (1999). *Pocket guide to service learning.* Clemson, SC: National Dropout Prevention Center.

Education Commission of the States. (2000, May). *Service-learning: An administrator's tool for improving schools and connecting with the community* (ECS Issue Paper SL-00-03). Denver, CO: Author. Retrieved June 11, 2004, from www.ecs.org/clearinghouse/14/33/1433.htm

Elmore, R. F. (1996). Getting to scale with good educational practice. *Harvard Educational Review, 66*(1), 1–26.

Eyler, J., & Giles, D. (1999). *Where's the learning in service-learning?* San Francisco: Jossey-Bass.

Eyler, J., Giles, D., & Schmiede, A. (1996). *Practitioner's guide to reflection in service-learning.* Nashville, TN: Vanderbilt University Press.

Furco, A. (2002). Is service-learning really better than community service? A study of school service program outcomes. In A. Furco & S. Billig (Eds.), *Service-learning: The essence of the pedagogy* (pp. 23–50). Greenwich, CT: Information Age.

Gardner, H. (1983). *Frames of mind: The theory of multiple intelligences.* New York: Basic Books.

Gardner, H. (1997, September). Multiple intelligences as a partner in school improvement. *Educational Leadership*, pp. 20–21.

Kolb, D. (1984). *Experiential learning: Experience as the source of learning and development.* Upper Saddle River, NJ: Prentice Hall.

Learn and Serve, Corporation for National and Community Service. (1995). [Definition of service-learning]. Retrieved April 11, 2005, from www.learnandserve.org/about/service_learning.html

Levine, M., & Duckerman, D. (2004, April). Getting down on self-esteem. *Youth Today: The Newspaper on Youth Work, 13*(4), 1, 6–8.

Lickona, T. (1991). *Educating for character: How our schools can teach respect and responsibility.* New York: Bantam.

Melchior, A., & Bailis, L. N. (2002). Impact of service-learning on civic attitudes and behaviors of middle and high school youth: Findings from three national evaluations. In A. Furco & S. Billig (Eds.), *Service-learning: The essence of the pedagogy* (pp. 23–50). Greenwich, CT: Information Age.

Mendler, A. (2000). *Motivating students who don't care.* Bloomington, IN: National Education Service.

National Training Laboratories. (n.d.). *The learning pyramid.* Retrieved April 11, 2005, from www.acu.edu/cte/activelearning/whyuseal2.htm

Pittman, K., & Irby, M. (1996). *Preventing problems or promoting development: Competing priorities or inseparable goals?* Baltimore: International Youth Foundation.

RMC Research Corporation. (2002, December). *Sustaining service-learning in K–12 schools.* Retrieved April 11, 2005 from www.servicelearning.org/resources/fact_sheets/k-12_facts/sustaining/index.php

RMC Research Corporation. (2003, January). *Why districts, schools, and classrooms should practice service-learning.* Retrieved April 11, 2005, from www.service learning.org/resources/fact_sheets/k-12_facts/why/index.php

Scales, P., Blyth, D., Berkas, T., & Kielsmeier, J. (2000, August). The effects of service-learning on middle school students' social responsibility and academic success. *Journal of Early Adolescence, 20*(3), 331–358.

Scales, P., & Roehlkepartain, E. (2004). *Community service and service-learning in U.S. public school, 2004: Findings from a national survey.* St. Paul, MN: National Youth Leadership Council.

Search Institute. (n.d.). *Research on the 40 developmental assets.* Retrieved April 26, 2005, from www.search-institute.org/research/assets/

Sigmon, R. (1996). The problem of definition in service-learning. In R. Sigmon and colleagues, *The journey to service-learning.* Washington, DC: Council of Independent Colleges.

Silcox, H. C. (1995). *A how to guide to reflection* (2nd ed.). Holland, PA: Brighton Press.

Sunburst Communications. (2000). *How not to fight* [Videotape]. Pleasantville, NY: Author.

Switzer, G., Simmons, R., Dew, M., Regalski. J., & Wang, C. (1995, November). The effect of a school-based helper program on adolescent self-image, attitudes, and behavior. *Journal of Early Adolescence, 15*(4), 429–455.

Tai-Seale, T. (2000). Service-learning: Historical roots, present forms, and educational potential for training health educators. *Journal of Health Education, 31*(5), 256–261.

Thomsen, K. (2004). Positive youth development: If schools were like baseball teams! *Reclaiming Children and Youth, 13*(2), 80–84.

Westat, R. (1999). *Service-learning and community services in K–12 public schools.* National Center for Education Statistics: Statistics in Brief (NCES 1999–043). Washington, DC: U.S. Department of Education.

Index

CORWIN PRESS

The Corwin Press logo—a raven striding across an open book—represents the union of courage and learning. Corwin Press is committed to improving education for all learners by publishing books and other professional development resources for those serving the field of PreK–12 education. By providing practical, hands-on materials, Corwin Press continues to carry out the promise of its motto: **"Helping Educators Do Their Work Better."**